# YOUTH CLUBS

## A Catalyst for Rural Community Development in Tripura

DR. MD. JIAUL ISLAM CHOWDHURY
& DR. ADITI NATH

INDIA • SINGAPORE • MALAYSIA

ISBN
Hardcase 979-8-89610-312-7
Paperback 979-8-89556-021-1

# Contents

**Contents**

Contents

# Preface

This research attempts to identify the indispensable role of youth clubs in the tapestry of rural development in the Gomati District of Tripura. The district with its rich cultural heritage and unique socio-economic characteristics provides an excellent foundation for exploring the role of youth clubs in fostering community resilience and development. To conduct this research, local leaders, youth, and community stakeholders worked together and generously shared their knowledge and experiences which helped to understand the functions, programs, problems, and challenges of youth clubs.

The study explored the multifaceted functions of youth clubs, ranging from promoting civic engagement and social cohesion to developing leadership abilities and entrepreneurship. It is clear from the findings that the youth clubs are vital arenas for education, empowerment, and collective action rather than just being places for recreational activities. This book provides a thorough examination of the effects these clubs have on both individual members and the larger community by combining qualitative and quantitative research methods.

The study examined various problems that youth club faces while putting their programmes into action. These difficulties include staffing capacity, motivation for community service, community mobilization skills, coordination & cooperation with line departments, financial matters, etc. Additionally important barriers such as community involvement, professional skills and community engagement, networking, managerial challenges, and strategic planning were noted. The research also highlighted that government organizations in the Gomati district are actively supporting youth clubs through various initiatives for their promotion in different aspects.

The study will be useful to educators, community organizers, policymakers, and nongovernment organizations seeking to harness the potential of youth in rural areas. By shedding light on the success and struggle of youth clubs in the process of rural community development, the research aims to inspire further initiatives that promote active participation and sustainable development.

# Chapter – 1

# Introduction

Rural community development and social change are strongly influenced by young people. Rural community development aims to empower individuals to realize their potential, address problems, and ultimately make better use of resources to uplift their lives. Community development includes self-help, mutual support, neighbourhood development, integration, and the development of political decision-makers (Smith, 2006). If youth are to learn how to be productive members of society, they need to be fully involved in community change efforts. This has forever been the core value (Nitzberg, 2005). Because of their sheer numbers, youth participation in neighborhood programs is crucial because it provides an endless opportunity to develop a younger workforce that can accelerate financial development, primarily contribute to public security, exercise authority, and encourage social advancement within their organizations.

Young people offer a significant opportunity for development, particularly in developing nations. To bring about rapid progress for a nation, this segment of the populace would be required to harness, accelerate, skilful, & updated. The main piece of the populace comprises young people, who are energetic, imaginative, and dynamic. Youth, who exhibit strong enthusiasm, inspiration, and will, is the most crucial human resource for fostering a nation's financial, social, and political development.

India at present has the most elevated extent of youngsters in the world, and this pattern is supposed to go on for the following 20 years. India is the youngest of the populous nations because 34.8% of its total population was under the age of 18 at the time of the 2011 census. The size of a nation's youth population determines its growth potential and capability. If utilized appropriately, the youth's enthusiasm and energy have the potential to significantly influence public opinion and national progress. Moreover, if these youth are encouraged to form youth clubs then it could have a positive impact on the community. Youth clubs also known as community-based organizations have been actively functioning at the grassroots level. It is the youth club which gives a platform to the youth of a specific area to get nearer, assemble, converse and design exercises for their improvement and society at large. The members of the youth club voluntarily engage themselves in need based programmes at the local level by channelizing the resources of Government and non-government sector.

In case of any emergencies, it is the community people who have to respond to the crisis immediately. But the unorganized community follows a community power structure, community dynamics need a constructive approach to organize the people before exercising any developmental plan in that community, and their youth clubs play an important role as they are well conversant with social structure, social system, culture, and need of the community. It has been observed in the literature that many youth clubs have undertaken community development activities in rural areas and have created an impact on their socioeconomic development but their services are yet to be recognized at a larger scale. Thus, the study endeavoured to comprehend the role of youth clubs in community development and to identify the problems and challenges they confront while implementing the programs at Gomati District of Tripura.

## 1.1 Conceptualising Youth

There is no globally settled upon meaning of youth. However, for statistical purposes, the United Nations defines "youth" as individuals between the ages of 15 and 24 regardless of any other definitions adopted by Member States. This definition was arisen for planning of International Youth Year (1985) and was supported by the individuals from General Assembly in its goal 36/28 of 1981. According to year book of UN on demography, education, employment, and health, this definition serves as the foundation for all youth-related statistics. Thus, this measurably arranged meaning of youth demonstrates that individuals younger than 14 years are children.

The United Nations Secretariat acknowledges that distinct definitions of youth exist for a number of UN instruments, regional organizations, and entities. These differences are summarized in the following table:

| Organization | Age (years) |
|---|---|
| UN Secretariat/UNESCO/ILO | Youth:15–24 |
| UN Habitat (Youth Fund) | Youth:15–32 |
| UNICEF/WHO/UNFPA | Adolescent: 10–19<br>Young people: 10–24<br>Youth: 15–24 |
| UNICEF/The Convention on Rights of the Child | Child under 18 |
| The African Youth Charter Youth | 15–35 |

Many nations also impose restrictions on minors regarding the age at which a person is entitled to equal treatment under the law, which is frequently referred to as the "age of majority." In many countries, this age is normally 18 on the grounds that, by then, an individual is viewed as a grown-up. However, the operational definition of the term "youth" in each nation is influenced by a variety of socio-cultural, institutional, economic, and political factors.

In India, the expression "youth" was characterized in the National Youth Policy 2003 as an individual between the ages of 13 and 35. However, in accordance to Youth Policy 2014, ages between 15 and 29 are considered to be young. This study uses the policy's definition of youth from 2014.

**1.1.1 Youth and Sustainable Developmental Goals (SDGs):** The 17 Sustainable Development Goals (SDGs) are adopted by the United Nations as part of the 2030 Agenda for ensuring sustainable development. These 17 goals were set to address the challenges faced by individuals such as poverty; hunger; good health and wellbeing; quality education; gender equality; clean water and sanitation; affordable and clean energy; decent work and economic growth; Industry, innovation and infrastructure; reduced inequality; sustainable cities and communities; responsible consumption and production; climate action; life below water; life on land; peace, justice and strong institutions; partnerships for the goals. These goals are to be achieved by 2030 by the active participation of individuals, communities and youth.

The 2030 Agenda is based on inclusivity and leaving no one behind philosophy, emphasising youth as the critical stakeholders in the pathway of sustainable development. Thus, knowledge, energy, and innovative spirit of the youth to be promoted by involving and engaging them in decision making process and in implementing different initiatives to create a significant and meaningful impact in addressing global challenges appropriately. Youngsters are a significant resource for social change, and the main agent for bringing economic and technological advancement. They are undertaking noble initiatives, driving social advancement, and motivating political change, thereby making their own communities resilient. Youth are not only the primary force behind the successful implementation of SDGs but also they are going to experience directly the results of such as the young leaders of today or tomorrow.

Therefore, it is of utmost importance for the youth to take part in the global visions set for the future and to keep them informed about the 2030 Agenda for Sustainable Development Goals and establish forums for having discussion, and foster active engagement. Considering the fact that young generations are the foundations of any economy, country like India has to reinforce strategies that target youngsters and make suitable youth improvement programs at different levels. Such approach would require a proper data base on youth to recognize the gaps, delineate the necessities and for adopting suitable intercessions. The dependable information will make it easier to create need based policies and programmes and will also make it possible to develop measurable indicators and serve as benchmarks for evaluating progress. Therefore, Youth in India was first published as a one-time publication by the Ministry in 1998, followed by its second and third editions in 2006 and 2017.

**1.1.2 Youth at International Sphere:** It was because of United Nations efforts in terms of formulating policies, many developing nations could focus on youth. However, youth centred initiatives have been in place since 1946 by UNESCO. Afterward, office of the High Commissioner for Human Rights set the overall plan for affirmation and acknowledgment by member Nations, Non-Government Associations, and Youth Developments in the General Assembly resolution 2307(XX) of 7 December 1965, to be explicit Declaration on Promotion among Youth of the Ideals of Peace, Shared Regard and Understanding between People groups.

The United Nations General Assembly selected “Participation, Development, and Peace” as the theme for the 1985 International Youth Year. It has drawn the consideration of the world to the significance of young person’s commitment to improvement. Around the same time, the General Assembly likewise supported the rules for additional preparation and fitting subsequent in the field of youth strategy arranging. These rules are critical in light of the fact that they center on youngsters overall, not as a single demographic category comprised of various subgroups.

The Unified Countries reinforced its obligation to youngsters by guiding the worldwide local area’s reaction to the difficulties youth will look in the following thousand years in 1995, on the event of the 10th commemoration of the Global Youth Year. It accomplished this by executing the World Program of Action for Youth in the Year 2000. This World Program aims to make nations more open to youth’s expectations that they are essential to the arrangement rather than the problem and their aspirations for a better world. Resolution 64/134 of the United Nations General Assembly, which declared 2009 the Year of Youth, demonstrated the importance that the international community places on incorporating youth-related issues into development plans at the global, regional, and national levels.

Through specifically designed programs, the United Nations focuses primarily on youth. From August 12, 2010, to August 11, 2011, the International Year of Youth was commemorated with the theme “Dialogue and Mutual Understanding.” It embraces a degree of exercises to drive youth improvement including supporting intergovernmental framework making, planning legitimate evaluation, and expanding the sensibility of the UN’s work in youth improvement by reinforcing worked with effort and trade among UN substances through the Inter-Agency Network on Youth Development (IANYD). Representatives from UN agencies whose work is relevant to youth issues were selected to form the organization in February 2010.

The 2013 Workplace of the Secretary-General's Emissary on Youth demonstrates that the United Nations continues to prioritize youth as one of its primary concerns. Its first Emissary on Youth was appointed in January 2013, with the responsibilities of bringing the United Nations' work with and for youth closer to them, planning UN initiatives on youth development, working on the UN's response to youth needs, and advocating for youth improvement needs and privileges. The overall prerequisites of the Work environment of the UN Secretary-General's Messenger on Youth are composed by the need of the World Program of Development for Youth and the need locale of the UN Design.

**1.1.3 Youth at National Sphere:** The Ministry of Youth Affairs & Sports was initially established under the name Department of Sports when the IX Asian Games were held in New Delhi in 1982. It was renamed as the Department of Youth Affairs & Sports in 1985 as part of the International Youth Year celebrations. It became a Ministry on May 27, 2000. Thus, the services have been bifurcated into the Division of youth affairs and the Department of Sports since 30 April, 2008 having two secretaries.The subjects managed by these two divisions are illustrated in the request of the Govt. of the 1961 India Business Allocation Rules.

It was the responsibility of the Department of Youth Affairs to formulate policies, programs, and regulations for the development of the youth. To maximize youth's creative and constructive potential, the Department of Youth Affairs pursues dual goals like personality-building and nation-building, i.e., developing youth's personalities and involving them in a variety of activities aimed at nation-building. The Department has additionally perceived 'Adolescents' as a significant section of the youth and started functioning on youth-related issues like Education, employment and training, health, and family welfare. The services provided by the Department of Youth Affairs in this regard served as both a catalyst and a facilitator.

Realising the importance of active participation of the young people in economic growth by addressing youth unemployment in the country, the government formulated need-based policies and put forth various plans into action to make them accessible to the youth who constitutes more than a quarter of the population. The following is a brief description of the government's initiatives.

## 1.2 Unemployment Status of Youth

India had a high youth unemployment rate of 17.8% between 2017 and 2018. However, this rate dropped significantly to 12.9% in 2020-21, indicating that the employment situation for young people has improved over time. It is observed that in comparison to rural youth, urban youth are facing more unemployment issues which indicate that employment opportunities for youth are limited in urban areas. It features that female youth encountered a higher joblessness rate contrasted with male youth, reflecting gender disparity in job market. However, some improvement could observe in female unemployment situation during 2020-2021.

**1.2.1 Trends of Youth Unemployment-Global Perspective:** The world-wide unemployment rate of various age groups during the 2010-2021 as per ILO is presented below-

According to ILO definitions, the people ages 15−24 years are considered as "youth", while 'adults' are people aging between 25 years and over. According to ILO data, the world wide unemployment rate was around 13% during 2010 to 2019, with the exception of the years 2020 and 2021, the pandemic period. The data presented above though indicating some positive trends yet there is more to be done to address prevalent unemployment scenario. A multi faceted approach having education, training, placement, job creation, skill development etc. is required to improve employability (Labour & Employment Statistics, 2021).

Employment generation has always been a concern for government. Through the implementation of various employment generation programs, the government has taken various actions to generate employment in the nation are highlighted below-

| Sl.No | Schemes/ Programmes | Objective | Employment Generated |
|---|---|---|---|
| 1. | Pt. Deen Dayal Upadhyaya-Grameen Kaushlya Yojana – DDU-GKY | To reduce poverty by enabling the poor households to access gainful self-employment and skilled wage employment opportunities through placement-linked skill training program, launched | During last five years (2017-18 to 2021-22)<br>Candidates Trained: 6.78 lakh<br>Candidates Placed: 4.22 lakh |
| 2. | Pradhan Mantri Kaushal Vikas Yojana (PMKVY) | It is a Skill Certification Scheme, to enable a large number of Indian youth to take up industry relevant skill training, launched w.e.f. July 2015. | As on 07.03.2022<br>Candidates Trained: 1.35 crore Candidates Placed: 23.96 lakh |

| | | | |
|---|---|---|---|
| 3. | Pradhan Mantri Mudra Yojna (PMMY) | To fund the unfunded micro enterprises segment through a new financial inclusion initiative launched on April 8, 2015. | During 2021-22<br>No. Of PMMY Loans Sanctioned: 5.38 crore<br>Amount Disbursed: 3,31,402 crore |
| 4. | Pradhan Mantri Rojgar Protsahan Yojana (PMRPY) | To incentivize employers for creation of new employment launched w.e.f. August 2016. | As on 31.03.2022<br>Employees benefitted: 1.22 crore<br>Establishments benefitted: 1.53 lakh |
| 5. | Rural Self Employment Training Institutes (RSETIs). | Skill Development through Rural Self Employment Training Institutes (RSETIs) enabling a trainee to take bank credit and start his/her own micro-enterprise | As on 31.03.2022 (since April 2008)<br>Candidates Trained: 35 lakh Candidates Settled: 24.41 lakh Candidates Settled under Wage Employment: 2.36 lakh<br>Candidates Settled under Self Employment: 22.05 lakh |
| 6. | Mahatma Gandhi National Rural Employment Guarantee Act (MGNREGA) | It aims at enhancing the livelihood security of people in rural areas by guaranteeing 100 days of wage employment in a financial year to a rural household whose adult members volunteer to do unskilled manual work | During 2021-22<br>Employment Generated: 363.49 crore person days |
| 7. | Prime Minister's Employment Generation Programme (PMEGP) | It focuses on generating employment in the country by setting up of new self-employment ventures/ projects/ micro-enterprises in the nonfarm sector. | During 2021-22 (upto 15.03.2022) Employment generated: 6.91 lakh persons |

| | | | |
|---|---|---|---|
| 8. | Pradhan Mantri Garib Kalyan Rozgar Abhyan (PMGKRA) | To incentivize employers for creation of new employment along with social security benefits and restoration of loss of employment during Covid-19 pandemic, launched w.e.f. June 2020 and terminated on 22nd October, 2020. | Ended on 22nd October, 2020.<br>Employment Generated: 50.78 crore person days<br>Expenditure incurred: Rs. 39,293 crore |
| 9. | Atmanirbhar Bharat RojgarYojana (ABRY) | To incentivize creation of new employment opportunities during the COVID recovery phase by providing incentive to the employers of establishments, launched w.e.f. October 2020 and terminated on March, 2022. | As on 18.06.2022<br>Employees benefitted: 59.49 lakh<br>Establishments benefitted: 1.49 lakh |
| 10. | PM Street Vendors Atma Nirbhar Nidhi (PM SVA Nidhi) scheme | To give vendors access to affordable working capital loans which can help them to resume their livelihood activities post-countrywide lockdown (due to the pandemic), launched on June, 2020. Extended from March 2022 to till December 2024. | As on 31.03.2022<br>Applications sanctioned: 33.73 lakh Loan amount disbursed against 30.89 lakh applications. |

Source: Labour and Employment Statistics 2022

## 1.3 Youth Policy Initiatives

India did not have a national youth policy until 1987. Nonetheless, youth has perpetually been the worry of the Indian government. This is well demonstrated by the Union Government's various youth development initiatives following Independence, including the National Cadet Corps (NCC), National Service Scheme (NSS), Nehru Yuva Kendra Sangathan (NYKS), and financial assistance to Non-Government Organisations for youth development.

The Department of Youth affairs has initiated the process for National Youth Policy. After having far reaching discussions with the stakeholders a draft youth policy was formulated and was presented before State Ministers in charge of youth affairs in June 1987. Thereafter, in November and December 1988, a comprehensive National Youth Policy was prepared and was adopted by the Government with the consent of both the houses of parliament.

As per NYP, a Committee for National Youth Programmes (CONYP) was laid out with the Prime Minister as its Chairperson. As a result, the Department of Youth Affairs and Sports established a National Level Committee to develop the National Perspective Plan for the Youth in 1996-2020. The concerns identified by the committee for the youngsters are presented below-

(i) To look at the established, legitimate, social, and managerial arrangements that have an orientation on the situation of youth, their schooling, improvement, business, relaxation time, and diversion.

(ii) To recognize the situation of country's youth and suggest improvement measures for streamlining the youth and making them practically effective, monetarily useful, and socially coordinated.

(iii) To suggest steps and measures addressing health, education, employment, cooperation etc. for the betterment of the youth and strengthening of youth capacity.

**1.3.1 National Youth Policy 2003:** The National Youth Policy of 1988 was superseded by the National Youth Policy of 2003. In light of the current global situation, the policy was rewritten to encourage young people to adapt to the new situations and take part effectively and devotedly in the tasks of nation's development. Empowerment of youth in various facets of national life was the primary focus of the Policy. The definition of youth used in this policy included individuals between the ages of 13 and 35.

The goal of the policy is to make sure that youth development programs that emphasize community service, self-reliance, national integration, humanism, and social justice, as enshrined in our ancient scriptures, are implemented effectively. These programs also encourage personality development and citizenship skills. The National Youth Policy of 2003 had the following goals:

(i) To instill in the general youth an unwavering commitment to patriotism, national security, national integration, nonviolence, and social justice, as well as an abiding awareness of and adherence to the secular principles and values enshrined in the Indian Constitution;

(ii) To foster characteristics of Citizenship and commitment to service towards community among all segments of the young;

(iii) To advance mindfulness, among the young, in the fields of Indian history and legacy, expressions, and culture;

(iv) To facilitate the youth with meaningful educational and training opportunities and to make them accessible to information regarding employment, entrepreneurial and financial credit opportunities.

(v) To facilitate youth with health related information & services and to encourage youth to promote a social climate that firmly restrains the utilization of drugs and different types of substance abuse. Youth are expected to take drug de-addiction measures and mainstream the affected people by engaging them in sports.

**1.3.2 National Youth Policy 2014:** National Youth Policy 2014 reaffirms its commitment to the comprehensive advancement of India's youth so they can understand their maximum capacity and assist with building the country. The policy replaced NYP 2003 in 2014 after extensive discussions with all stakeholders. Youth in accordance to NYP 2014 is an individual ages between 15 to 29 years. The new policy identifies five objectives and priority areas to understand the vision of said policy are summed up through a below given table. Additionally the policy suggests interventions under all of the 11 areas of priority.

**Vision, Objectives, and Priority Areas of NYP 2014**

| Sl. No | Vision | Objectives | Priority Areas |
|---|---|---|---|
| 1. | **To empower youth of the country to achieve their full potential, and through them enable India to find its rightful place In the community of nations** | Create a productive workforce that can make a sustainable contribution toIndia's economic development | ▪ Education<br>▪ Employment & Skill Development<br>▪ Entrepreneurship |
| 2. | | Develop a strong and healthy generation equipped to take on future challenges | ▪ Health & Healthy lifestyle<br>▪ Sports |
| 3. | | Instill social values and promote community service to build national ownership | ▪ Promotion of social values<br>▪ Community Engagement |
| 4. | | Facilitate participation and civic engagement | ▪ Participation in Politics & Governance<br>▪ Youth Engagement |
| 5. | | Support youth at risk & create equitable opportunity for all | ▪ Inclusion<br>▪ Social Justice |

Source: National Youth Policy 2014

## 1.4 Government Schemes / Programmes for Youth in India

From 2015 to 2016, ten schemes and programs for the benefit of youth were implemented by the Department of Youth Affairs and the Ministry of Youth Affairs and Sports. However, to enhance synergy and resource efficiency, the Department's entire scheme implementation has been merged into three schemes as of April 1, 2016. Table 1 provides the details of the merged schemes.

### Details of Restructured Schemes, 2016-17

| Name of Schemes (Before Restructuring) | Name of Schemes (After Restructuring) |
|---|---|
| Nehru Yuva Kendra Sangathan (NYKS) | Merged into a new 'umbrella' Scheme called"**RashtriyaYuvaSashaktikaran Karyakram (RYSK)**". |
| National Youth Corps (NYC) | |
| National Programme for Youth & Adolescent Development (NPYAD) | |
| International Cooperation | |
| Youth Hostels (YH) | |
| Assistance to Scouting & Guiding Organizations | |
| National Discipline Scheme (NDS) | |
| National Young Leaders Programme(NYLP) | |
| National Service Scheme (NSS) | National Service Scheme (NSS) |
| Rajiv Gandhi National Institute of Youth Development (RGNIYD) | Rajiv Gandhi National Institute of Youth Development (RGNIYD) |

**Rashtriya Yuva Sashaktikaran Karyakram (RYSK):** RYSK as a flagship programme was started under Department of Youth Affairs to assist youngsters with understanding their true capacity and add to country building. The following are the specifics of the scheme that fall under the umbrella scheme of Rashtriya Yuva Sashaktikaran Karyakram.

**Nehru Yuva Kendra Sangathan (NYKS):** One of the largest organizations for young people in the world is Nehru Yuva Kendra Sanghatn established in 1972. The sanghatan is available in 623 Districts. The very objective of NYK is to get youngsters engaged with activities that form a country and foster their personality and leadership skills. The main focuses of

NYKs are on health & family welfare, education, sanitation, awareness on social issues, environment protection, etc. Youth associated with NYK are not only socially sensitised but also inclined to volunteer themselves for societal development work. Different projects of NYKs are carried out through the involvement of youth clubs affiliated under NYK. The country has 1.79 lakh youth clubs with 35.06 lakh members starting around 2020-2021.

**Core Programmes of NYKS**

- Youth Club Development Programme
- Training on Youth Leadership and Community Development
- Promotion of Sports: Sports Material to Youth Clubs and Assistance for organisation of Sports Meets.
- Skill Up-gradation Training Programme
- Promotion of Folk Art and Culture and YuvaKriti
- Observance of Days of National and International importance
- District Youth Convention
- Awards to Outstanding Youth Clubs
- Mahatma Gandhi YuvaSwachhtaAbhiyanevemShramdanKaryakram
- YuvaAadarsh Gram VikasKaryakram.

The aforementioned core programmes are same to all 623 districts where NYKs are in existence. Out of the total number of programmes, youth clubs ensures to organise minimum two programmes exclusively for the women.

**Other Programmes/Activities of NYKS**

- National Integration Camps
- Youth Leadership and Personality Development Programme
- Life Skill Training for Adolescents.
- Adventure Camps
- Tribal Youth Exchange Programme

**National Youth Corps:** NYKS is currently carrying out the National Youth Corps program, which was first implemented in 2010–11. The goal of the scheme is to create a well behaved and committed group of young people who have the drive and motivation to take on the task of i) nation-building, ii) inclusive growth (both social and economic), iii) community points for information and knowledge dissemination, iv) peer educators, v) improving public ethics, honesty, and the dignity of work. Youth between the ages of 18 and 29 are recruited as volunteers for up to two years to participate in block-level nation-building projects. Against the target of 13,206 volunteers in 2020-21, 12,245 volunteers have been deployed in 706 districts.

**National Programme for Youth and Adolescent Development (NPYAD):** The NPYAD is a part of RYSK scheme under which monetary help is given to Government/non-Government organizations for taking up activities for youth and teenagers.

The beneficiaries under the scheme are youth aging between 15-29 years and adolescents aging 10-19 years.

1. Youth Leadership and Personality Development Training;
2. Promotion of National Integration
3. Promotion of Adventure; Tenzing Norgay National Adventure Awards
4. Development and Empowerment of Adolescents (Life Skills Education, Counselling, Career Guidance, etc.)
5. Technical and Resource Development (Research and Studies on Youth issues, Documentation, Seminars/ Workshops)

**National Young Leaders Programme (NYLP):** The NYLP programme began operations in December 2014 to help young people acquire leadership skills. The programs are designed to help young people become better leaders so that they can live up to their full potential and help build the country. The Program aims to bring young people to the forefront of development and inspire them to attain excellence in their respective fields. It hopes to equip the colossal youth energy for public structure. Individual aging 15-29 years are the beneficiaries of scheme.

**Youth Hostels (YH):** Hostels for youth are constructed to provide young people with the opportunity to see and experience the country's diverse cultural heritage and to encourage youth travel. Both the Central and State Governments collaborated on the construction of the Youth Hostels. All sorts of expenses related to development are borne by the central government and the state government provides land liberated from cost with water supply, power and roads. Youth Hostels can be found in a variety of settings, including tourist destinations, educational establishments, areas of historical and cultural significance, and so forth. For young people, youth hostels provide quality lodging at an affordable price. All together 84 Youth Inns have been worked the country over.

**Assistance to Scouting and Guiding Organizations:** Assistance to Scouting and Guiding Organizations began at the beginning of the 1980s for the promotion of movement on Scouts and Guides throughout the country. This is a worldwide development that expects to impart in young boys and young girls a feeling of nationalism, self-assurance, and idealism. The activities of the organisation are focussed to adult literacy, environment protection, health education, and sanitation & hygiene maintenance.

**National Service Scheme (NSS):** NSS was first carried out in 1969 with the essential objective of aiding student youth to develop their personalities and character through voluntary service. The purpose of the National Service Scheme is to 'Education through Service". The ideals of Mahatma Gandhi serve as inspiration for the NSS's ideological orientation. The motto of NSS is "NOT ME, But rather YOU." An NSS volunteer gives priority to the "community" than "oneself." The following qualities and skills are intended to be developed among the youth volunteers by NSS.

To gain an understanding about the community in which youth volunteers of NSS works and to figure out their situation in the context of that community

To learn about the problems and needs of the community and get student youth volunteers involved in exercises for solving problems.

(i) To develop a feeling of social and community obligation within themselves;
(ii) To utilize their insight in identifying reality-oriented problem solving strategies to address community & individual problems.
(iii) To learn how to get people in the community to participate;
(iv) To develop democratic principles and leadership skills;
(v) To foster the ability to meet crises and catastrophic events; and
(vi) To promote integration of the nation and maintain social harmony.

**Rajiv Gandhi National Institute of Youth Development (RGNIYD):** The Ministry of Youth Affairs and Sports recognised Rajiv Gandhi National Institute of Youth Development (RGNIYD) as Institute of National Importance by the 2012 RGNIYD Act. Subsequently in 2008, RGNIYD ensured the status of "Deemed to be University" by the Ministry of Education. RGNIYD is an important resource centre because of its many facets. It offers postgraduate programmes that cover a variety of aspects related to youth advancement, conducts training and capacity-building programs in the field of youth development, offers outreach and extension programs all over the country. The Institute is the nation's leading organization for activities involving youth and serves as the Ministry's think tank. It works together closely with the organisations like NSS, NYKS and other public youth associations in its ability as the most noteworthy organization. RGNIYD has an extensive association with different organisations functioning for the government assistance to improve youngsters by acting as a mentor.

To review the continuous status of progress among the youngsters of India that can allow an opportunity to develop youth development through the affirmation of their necessities and capacities, RGNIYD has drawn out the India Youth Development Index.The multi-layered properties that show progress in youth improvement at the sub-public, or state, level are the objective of the YDI. The index analyzes the variables that influence youngsters between the ages of 15 and 29 across six key domains like work, health, political and civic engagement as well as social inclusion.

## 1.5 Conceptualizing Youth Club

Youth Club is a village level organisation endeavoring towards the accomplishment of shared objectives and goals of the community. It is created, run, and managed by young people for the benefit of the community as a whole and young people in particular. The individuals from the Young Club comprise both male and female youth. By chance if any club has only females as members are known as Mahila Mandal which pertake similar status for overall practice purpose.

- Youth Clubs are possessed and constrained by youngsters who benefit straightforwardly from them. The basic features of a Young Club are:
- Individuals as members ought to be between the ages of 13-35 years
- That Club's office bearers can only be members between the ages of 18 to 35.
- Regardless of class, caste, faith, gender, community, membership might be given to all youth.
- Youth should have a sense of belonging and a stake in their community because they may make significant contributions to their Club and community.
- Youth should recognize issues, conceptualize, execute arrangements, and assess their projects.

**1.5.1 Historical background of youth club: International Scenario:** There has been a lot of focused thought and work over the couple of years on the complicated issues of creating a better rural life. This work has highlighted the undeniable requirement to involve youngsters in development activities especially in rural development and extension projects.In 1896, the youth organisation was started in United States of America with the recommendation of Professor Liberty Hyde Bailly, Cornell University a pioneer association named 4-H club came into existence. This association empowered youth to undertake studies for agricultural development aiming to enhance their knowledge on the subject matter so that they began with their own ventures connecting to crop rising and eventually the youth started their organisation known as corn club. In this way with the foundation of the Smith-Switch Act in 1914, the 4-H clubs turned out to be important for the augmentation in farming and home financial aspects. The activities of the clubs are now carried out by the co-operative extension service of the Land Grant Universities in close cooperation with U.S.D.A.

**1.5.2 Historical Background of Youth club: National Scenario:** The scouting movement, which originated in Britain in 1909 and began in various locations throughout India between 1909 and 1911, is where the youth movement in India got its start. From that point forward it has been developing quickly and has turned into a cross country youth association. The object of Scout development being to deliver solid adolescents, truly, ethically and profoundly, and its point is to foster such characteristics which can transform them into praiseworthy individual, self-restraint, and confidence, willing and ready to serve the communities. The historical backdrop of rural youth association in India returns to year 1920, when a rural youth club was begun by the experts of VishwaBharti around Sri Niketan in West Bengal. Additionally in 1922, BhartiBalak Association was begun by late Dr. Tagore at Sri Niketan. The principal goals of this association were the physical, mental and social advancement of the individual and fostering their manual abilities spirit of community service.Later on in 1952, Kamal Dal association was begaun in U.P. The name was given by Allahabad Rural Organization in Hindi. By 1953, a number of organisations came into being and started organisingShramdanactivity.Mela, exhibition and rallies. The youth development program turned into a significant program of community development with the proposal of the Fifth development Commissioners Conference (1956). Through which the States were educated to arrange the rural youth clubs in the villages all through India. Before independence very little efforts were taken in this regard. The significance of putting together rural youth was visualised only after independence. In 1952, youth related matters could draw the attention of national policy.

In this way in 1953-54 endeavours were made in various parts of the country to organise the rural youth following 4-H clubs pattern. The significance of scientific study of rural youth, their concerns and solutions drew the consideration of planners.Gradually, the Lucknow Research and Action Institute launched a pilot venture to foster a model for rural youth association in six villages of Etawah and Bellia districts. In 1959, the national conference on community development was held in Mysore and it suggested the appointment of a Director of Youth program in each state. In 1960, the Community Development National Conference at Srinagar suggested that the village school teacher ought to bear the obligation of organising the youth programme for the whole neighbourhood youth. In July 1961, the yearly meeting of State Ministers of Rural Development and Panchayats at Hyderabad depicted the youth programmes as the imperative base for the Panchayat Raj Development. They recommended that the Panchayat association ought to reserve a particular amount for youth associations in the block. This meeting likewise gave lead to the formation of Co-ordinating committees at the central level for advancing an incorporated youth government assistance program.

The Public Youth Barricade was set in 1970 and was reconstituted in 1978. The principal capability of this board is to bring co-ordination amongst the different divisions of Central, State, Union territories and voluntary organisations working for the development of the youth and giving advices and guidance on the detailing of policies related to youth.

Gradually considering the importance of having a national level organisation providing opportunities to youth were felt and thus in 1972 Nehru YuvaKendras were established under Ministry of Youth Affairs & Sports aiming to form youth clubs at the grassroots level for nation building and community development.

**1.5.3 Need of Youth Club:** Youth Club gives young people in a specific area a place to get together, meet, talk about, and plan activities that help them and society grow. Through the establishment of Youth Clubs, the nation's greatest human resource 'youth' is channeled and mobilized for its development. Youth Clubs Enable the Young:

- To recognize the necessities and issues of the local area and give solutions by preparing the required resource.
- To bring a positive change among the young and the masses by instilling social, cultural, civic and national values.
- To instill poise of work, the soul of volunteerism, a feeling of responsibility, self-reliance and quality of good citizenship among the youth.
- To fight for social injustices and promote feeling of brotherhood followed by National Integration.

Youth club gives an opportunity to the youth for playing a vital role in building a strong nation. Youth Clubs can take up issues concerning the marginalised, disabled, downtrodden etc. in the society. Youth Clubs can impart public pride in adolescents and advance upsides of resilience, fellowship, sadbhavana, harmony, love, crew, secularism, a majority rules system, and solidarity. Youth clubs actively can take part in the activities like Sports, Culture, environment protection, charity etc of their choice. Getting engaged with such activities may develop their skill in terms of planning, decision making, monitoring & evaluation. Engagement of youth with the youth clubs may benefit an individual in various ways like.i) It may improve their identity, self esteem, emotional involvement and personality, ii) develop the life skills including leadership, public speaking, reliability, iii) improve communication skill, iv) reduce shyness, level of depression, loneliness (Scales and Leffort, 1999).

## 1.6 Community Development

Community people, who share common interests, jointly own or participate in something, share common characteristics, or have mutual relations can all be considered as members of a community. In other way community refers a physical location where people live, interact and engage themselves in various activities for development includes social, economic, infrastructure etc.

Community development is a process which involves the efforts of both the people and the government authorities. It is solely neither the responsibility of the government nor the community to improve the condition of the community. It requires a joint effort for uplifting socio-economic and cultural condition of the community with full participation and cooperation. In other way, community development empowers individuals and communities to actively contribute in the development of the nation along with the local communities (UNO).

Community development facilitates members to come together and take collective effort in generating solutions over problems. It assists to build the capacity of the community to address community issues which doesn't just happen; it takes conscious and conscientious effort to do one or more things to make the community better.

According to planning commission, community development is a method of rural extension by which the five year plan aims to begin the process of transforming the social and economic life of the villages. Self-help as an approach followed in community development which encourages the villagers to make developmental plans and execute those plans for the improvement of their own communities. In such circumstance, government's role remains limited to technical guidance and financial support as the objective of the CD is to promote self reliance at the individual level and make an individual self sufficient to witness their development. It encourages collective action within the community and facilitates setting up of people's institutions like Panchayat, cooperative societies and other development committees (GOI).

Enhancing the skills and knowledge of individuals and community at large is the focus of community development so that it can empower community members to actually address different difficulties and explore scopes effectively. Active involvement of the community inhabitants for planning, generating solutions and take action towards developing the community's social, economic, environmental, and cultural aspects is central to the concept of community development. It emphasizes the importance of community participation in decision making process and initiatives that are essential for any sustainable development effort. Community participation will promote a sense of ownership and commitment among the members of the community.

## 1.7 Rural Community Development

India is a country who lives in villages. A significant portion of the population of India is the inhabitants of rural areas. Thus, the rural society plays a pivotal role in moulding country's overall growth and development. People of rural India often confronts with issues related to poverty, unemployment and traditionalism which limits access to economic opportunities, health care and education. High unemployment and underemployment rates are a common problem in rural areas. This implies that many individuals in rural communities don't have stable positions or access to opportunities leading to income generation. Due to the limited opportunities and resources available in these areas, many rural Indians face a significant obstacle in achieving a normal or improved standard of living. To gain significant progress as a country, it is important to focus on the development of rural areas so as to address the issues hindering the development process.

It indicates that the people of rural India must be educated, aware about the new developments, and furthermore urged to take different kinds of new strategies for shaping community development programs effectively. Both education and awareness can help them understand and adapt to the changes and opportunities in society. Ensuring participation of rural communities in community development programmes is crucial and the programmes meant for rural development is designed to address many pertinent issues and problems which will ultimately lead to improvement of rural life. The aim of the community development programme is to enhance the social, economic and cultural aspects of the community and the ultimate goal of community development is to bring comprehensive development in village life which means along with addressing economic needs, other aspects like preserving cultural heritage and promoting social cohesion is addressed.

**1.7.1 Importance of Youth Engagement in Rural Community Development:** Engaging youth in community development is important because of the following reasons.

(i) Critical thinkers: Youth are regarded as critical thinkers because they can uncover contradictions and biases, identify barriers to change, and challenge the existing power structure.

(ii) Change-makers: Young people can act and get others to act for bringing a change in society.

(iii) Innovators: For bringing new points of view, youngsters frequently have direct information on and bits of knowledge about issues that are not open to grown-ups.

(iv) Communicators: Young people can take part in communicating the agenda for development to their companions and networks at local level, districts and countries.

(v) Leaders: Youngsters have the ability to impact change in their networks and countries when they are furnished with information on their freedoms and backing for creating administration abilities. Youth-led organizations and networks should be supported and strengthened because they assist young people, particularly marginalized youth, in developing civic and leadership skills.

**1.7.2 Rural Community Development through Youth Clubs in the Study Area:** Youth club act as a change agent in rural community development in India. Youth clubs are doing various kinds of program and services in society with youth and community people in developing countries like India. Some of the activities of the youth club are given below:

**Promoting volunteerism spirit among the youth:** The youth clubs of the district are playing a vital role in promoting volunteerism among the community people of Gomati District since its inception. Various activities were initiated voluntarily as a part of community development in the villages such as cleaning programs, awareness programs, Conflict resolution, Work camps etc. Youth club gives the inspiration of voluntary spirit and knowledge to the young people and strong participation in the program and service in the district. Many excellent examples have been set in the promotion of Voluntarism in the south Tripura district. Voluntarism and youth club are very much correlated and never be separated from one another.

**Spreading Education and Career Development programmes:** Youth clubs had been playing a great role in spreading Education (Formal and Non Formal) in Rural South Tripura in collaboration with the Line department and many educational projects have been carried out by the youth club in promoting nonformal education and general education in society. The youth club also start a coaching class for the weaker section of families who cannot afford tuition fees in the rural area. Many Youth Clubs are running private Primary Schools, Middle Schools, and High Schools in the district. Many Youth clubs are concerned with Career Development among young people, organizing various career development programs in Schools, Colleges, and village-level workshops in collaboration with the education department and Employment Exchange office in the district. Many youth clubs are starting career development sessions on Sports, and Indian Defense like CRPF, ARMY, BSF, SSC, etc pre-training on Army recruitment in the local area for creating interest among the Youth in defense service. Many other educational Tours, Field visits are also carried out by the youth club in the district.

**Agriculture Development:** Youth clubs are very closely working in the field of Agriculture and at large no youth are engaged in the Agriculture sector in the form of Farmers clubs under NABARD, more than 98 Farmers clubs are run by the youth club in the district and get various services from the government. Youth clubs are engaged in Flower Plantation, Rubber plantation, Cultivation, Insurance, preparation of cards, helping the beneficiaries to get loans, and other facilities like Power Tiller, Seed, Fertilizer, Training, and capacity development training programs for young people and farmers in the Agricultural field. Youth clubs play as a change agent in the promotion of Agriculture schemes and programs for the farmers in local areas and work as resource centres in the village.

**Livelihood initiatives:** Youth clubs makes a significant contribution towards livelihood promotion of the communities through various skill development training programs with the line department in the village. By doing skill development training, many youths, Women are maintaining their livelihood in the village, and creating employability in various farms, Some of the skill development training programs organized by youth clubs are Cutting & Tailoring, Beautician Courses, Computer Courses, EDP, Flower Farming, Fish Farming, Scientific Bricks Industry, Animal Husbandry, Knitting and Embroidery, bamboo Product, Vegetable Farming like Mushroom etc in collaboration with Line departments in the district. Many youth clubs are helping poor people in getting married, children's Homes, sending the lonely aged person to Old age homes, etc the district.

**Disaster Management:** Youth clubs are actively engaged in the field of disaster management in the district. Regularly youth clubs are organizing awareness programs on disaster management and mock drill with the line department like IRCS, District Disaster Cell, and NDRF in the district. Youth club plays a very important role in giving awareness to young people in the community by involving local stakeholder in the community. Youth club members are involved in the Block level, Subdivision, and District level committees very actively and act as a key role in spreading awareness of disasters in the village. Youth clubs also active role in Disaster like Flood, Land Slide, and Accident in saving lives and resources in the village and also in rehabilitation of people affected by any natural calamities in the district youth clubs are always on the front line to serve voluntarily in any kind of disaster in the district.

**SwachataEvamShramdaan:** Youth club have a regular programme on swachata and shramdaan for cleaning the local area, Market, School, Religious place, road side, Office, Health Centre, Sports ground, statue, important institutes. Youth clubs are playing a very active role in spreading awareness on importance of Swachata and Shramdaan in the village by doing Home visit, IEC materials like Leaflets, Motivational Videos in collaboration with various line department like NYK, Panchayat, DWS department, DistrictAdministration, IRCS, etc in the district. Youth clubs are also actively participated in Swachatapakhwara, Swachata Hi Seva and mobilized large no youth in promoting swachata activities and creating sense of responsibility to the young people and community participation in maintaining cleanliness and safety of individual and community as a whole in the district.

**Sports Culture:** Youth clubs are creating an environment of sports among the young people in the village. Various sports competition is organized by the youth club in the village and inspired the young people in participation of sports as a career in the community. Youth club also initiate couching /Training programme on various events like Football, Athletic, Volleyball, Gymnastic, Yoga, Adventure programme etc in collaboration with Sports department and State Council of sports in the district to motivate the youngsters towards the sports and change the mind set of young people in career opportunity as ports. Youth clubs are also promoting Yoga and Meditation among the children and youth by running Yoga centre in the village and train the young people and provide the opportunity to participate in the competition from this district

**Traditional Culture promotion:** Youth clubs are also promoting cultural activities among the young people in the village. Many youth clubs are running training centers for Folk dance, Folk songs for the young champ to learn the traditional culture like the Folk culture of the community. Youth clubs are participating in various completions in Folk culture in the district and outside the district. Youth clubs are also participating in the National Integration Camp and Youth Festival for the promotion of state traditional culture in the state-level and National level programs. The youth club also organized various workshops on Folk culture and how to preserve it in the society among the young people in collaboration with ICA, Tribal welfare department, Dance Academy, and Cultural association in the district.

**Skill Development and life skill:** Youth clubs are organizing various programmes related to skill development in the study area to address the issues concerning the youth and community people at large. These Skill development programs are organized in collaboration with NYK, RSETI, NABARD, SIPARD, KBIB/KBIC, DDUKVY, Minority Ministry, RD Blocks Panchayat, DIC, District Administration, Tata Trust, Team lease, Apollo Med skill Pvt. Ltd. Etc in the village. Many youths are participating long term skill development programs outside the district and state through youth clubs from this district and getting the opportunity of employment outside the state. Youth clubs are organizing various skill development training like Tailoring, Beautician Courses, Computer Courses, EDP, Flower Farming, Fish Farming, Scientific Bricks Industry, Animal Husbandry, Knitting and Embroidery, bamboo Product, Vegetable Farming like Mushroom, Local Need base training, House wiring, Mechanic, paper bag making, Broom making, Achar, paper making, Fast food training, Handicraft, Bamboo coiling products, etc for the young people in the village. This activity of the youth club is directly helping the young people in scaling the skill and capacity development of young minds and employability and self-enterprise in the district. It is one of the most prioritised areas of work for the youth clubs of the district to accelerate the capacity and innovative ideas of young people in the village.

**Entrepreneurship and rural self-employment:** Many youth clubs are promoting entrepreneurship programs in the village to involve the young people in creating self-employment and generate the potential of individuals in initiating enterprise in the local area. Youth clubs are running small-scale industries, Small enterprises to promote the youth club member and villages in the socio-economic upliftment of young people in society. Youth clubs organizes various EDP programmes in the village to sensitize the people on Entrepreneurship and ensures facilities from the government in entrepreneurship development in the district. RSETI is an important organisation for promoting the EDP programme in youth clubs. Youth clubs also help to fill up the form of PMEGP, Swabalamban to young people for getting subsidies in the rural area of the district.

**Environment safety:** Youth clubs play a very important role in an environment enrichment program in the district. Various programs like Tree plantation & care and support, sense of honor, Tree plantation competition, Plant distribution to villagers, Plastic free environment campaign, save water campaign swachatamakiwara, etc. are regularly organized by the youth club in the district. Various awareness programs on the plastic-free environment and safe water campaigns were organized in villages, schools, colleges, and panchayats regularly in the district. Some youth club initiates ownership mega tree plantation program in the district with the Forest department in the district.

**Participation in Local governance:** Youth club also play an important role in local governance. Youth club act as a potential agent in community development process especially in Gram Sabha, local panchayat in terms of programme selection and implementation in the village and youth club inspire the young leader in political participation and active role in implementing various programme and schemes for the community development in the district. Many youth club members are actively participated and elected as representative in local governance and committees in the local area for smooth implementation of programme in the district.

**Observation of National and International important days:** Most of the youth clubs are observing the National and international importance days in the village and conduct various a program like lectures and discussions on the importance of the days, the contribution of great personalities, Exhibitions, Sports programs, and public rallies in the local area. Youths are actively participating in the program and many youth clubs organized PrabhatPheri in the local area to motivate the public for its promotion. This type of program gives a new thought to the youth in the local area towards a sense of responsibilities and necessary in the community development process. A large no of youth felt motivated through this program in the village and are devoting themselves in the process of nation building and developed a sense of integrity and coexistence with all communities of the district.

**Health and Hygiene:** Health is also a very important area where youth clubs are strongly participating in spreading various information effectively in the villages. A program like immunization programs, health Camps, Awareness of Health & Hygiene, organ donation awareness programs, and the Promotion of Ayush and Homeopathy in society. A large no of youth is actively participating in various immunization programs with other stakeholders and Workers in the village more effectively. The youth club has a very important role in health besides this youth clubs are regularly organizing Health Camp, Blood Donation Camps, and awareness programs in the village. A large no of youth donated every year through youth club in the district and plays a very important stakeholder in the state in voluntary blood donation.

**Work Camp:** Youth Clubs are popular for voluntary activities in the community developments in many areas of youth in the south Tripura district for many decades. Youth club members organize work camps for the particular construction of assets of the community through the voluntary effort of large no youth for the local area needs without any help from the govt. or Non govt. agency. Youth Club has a long history of voluntary work in South Tripura. Many programs like the construction of a Road (Connecting), Bridge, lake, Construction of Youth Club building, Pond, Plantation, water Reservoir, etc in the district. Work camp helps to understand the importance of unity and integration, developing the sense of belongingness, Responsibility, and contribution of every member towards the objectives of togetherness and voluntary effort in the society.

**Youth Leadership Training programme:** Many youth clubs are organizing youth leadership training programs like day workshops, seminars, lecture programs on leadership qualities, Communication Skills, Flagship programs, swachata and Shramdaan, Environment, plastic, etc among youth in the village, schools, higher secondary, college in collaboration with line departments in the district and encouraging the young people in participating the various youth leadership program organized by NYK, SIPARD, Team Lease, etc. in the state.

**HIV/AIDS and Substance Abuse:** The youth clubs organizes awareness programs on HIV/ AIDS and use of substance in collaboration with State AIDS control society and the Targeted Intervention Project in the district. The youth club is acting like an awareness machine in the field of HIV/AIDS and a large no of youth were involved in awareness programs of HIV /AIDS in the village. Youth clubs are closely working with the Health Department and police and another stakeholder in controlling substance abuse among the youth in the district, many cases of coordination activities gives excellent results in controlling substance abuse and spreading awareness s program in the district.

Besides this many other activities are also rendered by youth club in the community development process in the village. Many youth club are self reliant and maintaining routine activities in many ways to develop our society at large and Youth club plays in very important role in potential human resource development in the society and create a sense of ownership in community development process among the youth in the village.

# Chapter – 2

# Literature Review

In the annals of community development, a significant turning point occurred in 1959 during an annual conference held in Mysore, India. It was here that the concept of engaging youth clubs in the implementation of community development programs emerged as a potentially powerful vehicle for transforming the traditional attitudes of rural communities. The idea was to create an environment conducive to the widespread adoption of modern technologies, thereby fostering rural development. Interestingly, examples from countries like the United Kingdom, The Netherlands, Denmark, Germany, and the United States highlighted the substantial contributions of youth to agricultural development as early as 1962 (Jones, 1981). In contrast, India was slower to embrace the notion of rural youth clubs and their associated activities, with parents and villagers initially displaying limited interest (Shukla, 1971).

Gradually rural youth clubs have come up with community development programmes but their performance could not reach to the satisfactory level of the masses (Rai 1965). The membership of the clubs was dominated by the persons having matriculation or above (Kumar 1966). Only educated youth enrolled as member in the youth clubs however, education had no direct association with effective working of youth clubs. The author upon undertaking an intimate study of the subject matter under consideration also found that youth club activities could not ensure full cooperation of the villagers and influence of political parties on youth club activities are one of the reasons for not achieving success (Laksmana and Vijayamohan 1968).

Thus, it became evident that the key attributes or crucial facets of a successful youth club must be necessarily rooted in its non-political, non-religious, and non-sectarian character (Singh, 1963). These foundational attributes being considered as indispensable have resultantly been deemed as fundamentally vital for building an effective youth club (Ramamurthy, 2006). In this relevant context, fostering a positive attitude among youth emerged as a critical factor in making these clubs functional (Patel et al., 2011).

Recognising the untapped potential fundamentally inherent in channelling the energy and enthusiasm of this young demographic for constructive purposes, it was clear that India could position itself among the prosperous nations of the world. Moreover, linking youth clubs with local institutions such as panchayats and cooperatives was seen as a pathway to national development (Singh, 1977). Furthermore, an effective study by (Tripathi et al., 2018) revealed that a majority of rural youth harboured dissatisfaction with their rural lifestyle due to the scarcity of basic necessities. The study further indicated that dissatisfaction often propelled the rural youth towards migration as a means of seeking social and economic betterment, thereby diverting their involvement in community work. Consequently, many viewed migrations as an avenue for social and economic improvement, which, in turn, led to reduced active engagement in community work.

The work of the rural youth henceforth must be re-thought considering the importance of rural youth as the fundamental segment of the population. The predicament faced by rural youth was exacerbated by their limited access to land and basic necessities, encompassing food, education, healthcare, and employment (Albal&Koujalagi, 2018).These challenges positioned rural youth as one of the most disadvantaged groups, with their training opportunities significantly constrained in comparison to those available in urban areas. These factors collectively contributed to the inexorable trend of young people migrating to urban areas, diverting their potential contributions to rural community development (Albal&Koujalagi, 2018).The background study underlined the importance of conducting thematic reviews on i) Rural Community development,ii)Social Capital and Community Development; iii) Youth Clubs/ Community Based Organisations in Rural Community Development; iv) Challenges of Youth Clubs, to gain better understanding on the stated problems by identifying the gaps based on which the objectives of the study have been formulated.

## 2.1 Rural Community Development

Pyakuryal. K (1970) offered a valuable insights into the nuanced relationship between community development and rural development. The literature distinguished community development as a distinctive approach to rural development, characterised by a focus on human interactions within the specifications of geographical boundaries. In contrast, the literature also enumerates that rural development assumes a broader ecological perspective. The author appropriately connotes that while, human settlements are dispersed throughout both rural and urban areas, it is in the rural context that dedicated development programs are crafted. These initiatives confront multifaceted challenges, including rural poverty, illiteracy, poor health, regional disparities, and power imbalances. The overarching goal of rural development therefore, persists to enhance the quality of life for those residing in rural areas.

Kumar (1981) stated that rural development is “a movement designed to promote better living conditions for the whole community through active participation of the people themselves”.

Successful rural development hinges on the genuine embrace of its principles by the local populace. According to Decree No. 4 of 1986, which established the Directorate of Food, Roads, and Rural Infrastructure (DFRRI), rural development is a complex process. It involves carefully identifying rural needs and effectively mobilizing human and intellectual resources to meet those needs. These requirements encompass various aspects of rural life including sustenance, raw materials, essential infrastructure like roads, water supply, electricity, educational institutions, and healthcare facilities. The ultimate aim goes beyond mere provisions; it strives to foster economic and social engagement within these communities,cultivating self-reliance as well as nurturing the growth of robust local economies.

Obot (1989) while focusing his research towards the domain of rural community development noted within the scope of the literature thatthe degree or quantum of the relevant subject that is rural development could be measured or understood by analysing the growth, development or work in the areas of roads, water supply, housing, electricity, building of model communities, access to quality education, improvisationin the delivery mechanisms of health care facilitiesand availability of food and agricultural products for the rural settlers. The author further reveals that the non-governmental organisations stand to play an intrinsic role in developing all the aforementioned indicators for rural community development since many decades in India.

Rural development exists as the indispensable core necessity for ensuring the complete development of the country. While, some of the adhoc or even the fragmented approaches incorporated for effectuating the rural development are working to bring some change and development however, such fragmented measures stand incapable to solve the fundamental challenge of rural poverty in absolute terms. The author wide the stipulated literature presses over the need for a comprehensive rural development policy and pooling of resource involving both man and materials to achieve the desired national goal (Devi 1997).

Jain (1997) through its literary contribution to the existing piece of knowledge opined that rural development had to be directed more specifically to benefit the rural poor. Authorwent on to emphasise thatfundamentally focusing on effectuating an effective planning which stands focused to directly eradicatethe poverty instead of relying upon the principle of trickling effect to trickle down growth, prosperity and identical subjects to the poor.

Datta (1998) pointed out a significant shift in the realm of rural India's grassroots development, one that gained momentum following the 73rd Amendment to the Indian Constitution. This amendment placed a renewed emphasis over critical issues such as the development, participation, as well as the empowerment of women community in the Indian Republic. Datta's perspective underscores that fundamental truth that is, for the true realisation of the success of grassroots development and the untiring efforts of decentralisation hinges upon the empowerment of rural communities.

Pearce (2000) stated that community development approach contains three key parts: collective empowerment, collective leadership and leading change through dialogue. According to the author, it's the need of hour to use community development approach at rural areas as well as urban areas where local people should be involved in all stages such as need assessment, planning and implementing the programs.

Ismail (2001) mentioned that Community development is a process of activities at community level that are planned and organized movements in a particular way so as to improve the standard of life of the community as means of social, economy, culture and environment through initiatives and functioning participation and with minimum external help.

S. N. Tiwary (2011) astutely noted a common misconception surrounding rural development, often conflating it with agricultural development. While acknowledging the pivotal role of agricultural development as the foundation for rural and industrial progress, the author went on to emphasise that it must not be viewed as an ultimate objective in itself. Indeed, the health and well-being of rural communities are intricately tied to agricultural productivity. However, it persists intrinsic to recognise that rural development encompasses a broader spectrum of factors than solely agricultural growth. Beyond agriculture, rural areas require attention in various domains, including infrastructure development encompassing roads, water supply, housing, and the nurturing of cottage and small-scale industries. Equally significant are the processes and mechanisms for marketing local goods, facilitating trade, and enhancing economic resilience within these regions.

Saikia (2015) stated that rural development is concerned with economic growth and social justice; improving the living standard of the rural people, thereby providing adequate and quality social services with minimum basic needs to the people becomes essential. In the given literature, the author, through his valuable research writing, consequently underscored the multifaceted nature of rural development, where the twin goals of economic growth and social justice intertwine. This perspective, therefore, elevates the indispensable necessity of enhancing the living standards of rural communities, with a keen focus on providing essential as well as high-quality social services while also ensuring the fulfilment of the basic requirements of the people. The study undertaken by the author resonates with the imperative of rural development to serve as a conduit for not only economic progress but also social equity, affirming its role in fostering a better quality of life for rural inhabitants through comprehensive and inclusive strategies.

## 2.2 Social Capital and Community Development

Putnam et al., (1994) and Fukuyama (1996),postulated that social capital plays an intrinsic role in providing access to more information, increasing social cohesion, better civic engagement, reducing opportunistic behaviour, boosting political participation, government responsiveness and efficiency, reducing transaction costs, providing insurance against risk and uncertainties, and solving collective actions problems.

Durston, John (1999) explores the concept of "social capital" which encompasses the norms, institutions, and organisations that foster trust and cooperation within individuals in communities and society at a broader pedestal. According to Durston, establishing stable relationships based on mutual confidence and collaboration can even lead to reducing of transaction costs, creation of public goods, and the development of social actors indispensably intrinsic for the formation of sound civil societies as a whole.

The article by Labonte (1999) navigates the current discourse surrounding social capital, which has emerged as a prominent but controversial concept. It underscores the lack of consensus regarding its definition and the pressing need for theoretical development and measurement. Health promoters and other stakeholders are grappling with the challenge of adapting their strategies to accommodate this still-debated notion. The article contends that social capital is not an inherent entity but rather a product of selective social relations that align with the ideologies of particular theorists or researchers. For proponents of neoliberal, market-driven ideologies, social capital serves as a means to foster economic growth and compensate for the erosion of public services. Conversely, those inclined toward social justice and communitarian ideologies perceive social capital as an end in itself, necessitating robust state intervention to counter market-induced inequalities. Community development is identified as one among various state interventions aimed at mitigating disparities arising from market forces. The article suggests that social capital, while potentially valuable, should be wielded cautiously as a strategic construct, avoiding the risk of undermining previous efforts in the realms of empowerment and community capacity. By critically engaging with the contemporary fascination with "social capital" and focusing on the ongoing debate surrounding its definition and measurement, the inclusion of this manuscript within the scope the current literature review stands appropriate.

The research paper explores into the arena of evolving recognition of social capital as a dynamic resource with the potential to both facilitate and impede social actions. The manuscript focuses its lens on a village community in North India. Undertaking the research within its historical context, the article meticulously scrutinises the intricate processes underpinning the formation of the social capital. It further scrutinises the profound impacts of macro-structural changes on social capital, and goes on to explore about social capital's pivotal role in the broader realm of development. Notably, the research paper underscores the delicate interplay between formal and informal institutions, thereby emphasising that when the two entities clash, collective action stands severely hampered. Interestingly the article also suggests that a purposeful approach could be engineered to render the formal and informal institutions complementary and synergistic, which henceforth would effectively harness the social energy for the fundamental objective of development (Dhesi, 2000).

Annie E. Casey (2004) explain that social capital for communities fundamentally makes a notional reference to establishing trust-based networks the scope of which does not remain limited to constituting strong connections, never the less it also extends to bolstering the quality of such relationships within families, communities as well as organisations within the society. This fundamentally persists as the intrinsic as well an underlying ingredient determining healthy families and also building social capital among the communities.

Social capital plays a vital role in driving collective action for community development, a force that often surpasses the mere acquisition of economic resources. In this context, collective action signifies the unity of residents in their efforts to combat the obstacles, prejudices, and disparities that have weakened their influence in impoverished areas. It's important to note that research in community development underscores the intrinsic importance of collective action as an indispensable process for empowering community groups and fostering self-reliance. This process imbues the community with the strength and resilience needed to surmount challenges and chart a path toward a more prosperous future (Rubenson, 2005; Rubin, 2000; Wilkinson, 1991).

Alan Kay (2006) through a research project, carefully explored and defined the elusive concept of social capital in a study called "CONSCISE", examining the complexity of social capital and what it means more in socio-economic and community affairs. Later, a thorough investigation of methods began to investigate. The article then revealed several key findings, focusing on the critical role that social capital plays in underpinning ongoing socioeconomic and community development. As the story unfolds, it becomes clear that this research effort is not just an academic exercise but a practical journey into the heart of social relations. The article skilfully concludes by clarifying policy implications, offering a strategy for harnessing the power of social capital within the complex fabric of community development. Essentially, it transforms the abstract concept of social capital into a tangible and actionable resource for social improvement and well-being.

In the valuable research-based manuscript of Teshanee Williams, Jamie McCall, Maureen Berner, and Anita Brown-Graham (2022), social capital emerges as a pivotal asset with the potential to transform communities. While researchers have recently shifted their focus to explore how bonding and bridging social capital contribute to organizational success, the precise mechanisms governing organizational social capital remain shrouded in mystery. Within the realms of this academic exploration, it is suggested that both expressive and instrumental actions play integral roles in elucidating the impact of social capital. By synthesizing these concepts, the study delves into the intricate role of social capital within Community Development Organizations (CDOs).

The manuscript offers a comprehensive overview of social capital's application as a development tool and endeavours to pave the way for a more interdisciplinary framework. It goes on to delve into instances wherein communities have created and assessed social capital, extract cross-disciplinary insights, examine empirical evidence indicating causal relationships, and illustrates this synergy through three compelling examples: the influence of the built environment, migration patterns, and entrepreneurship on social capital and community development. The research-based article concludes by proposing a conceptual model which integrates all facets of Community Capitals into a holistic framework, advocating for a systemic perspective that recognizes the interplay among various elements, akin to the ecological "law of the minimum" where limiting factors constrain overall growth (Halstead et al., 2022).

## 2.3 Youth Clubs/ Community Based Organisations in Rural Community Development

Singh (1983) highlighted in his study that establishing rural youth clubs in villages is one of the successful approaches of organising rural youth. Author stated that the projects related to socio-economic development undertaken by the youth clubs contributes significantly for community development. The study suggested that the club members must be provided with training and other required facilities which keep them motivated for work. Organising Short term training courses, setting up of skill demonstration centre for the youth and the villagers have been recommended in the study.

Rajasekhar (1987) viewed that different evaluation studies undertaken by Government and other agencies time to time on youth have clearly indicated that the rural youth as a group are shy to take part in the rural development programmes. The author suggested undertaking appropriate measures to give better exposure to the youth so that they feel financially secured and gain interest to work for the community.

According to Anonymous (1992), the primary reason for which youth power is getting wasted are due to absence of wider inter linked network for youth organisation and proper guidance and training. Thus, it gives the base for low participation of rural youth in development activities. Therefore, the author emphasized the need for conducting systematic research to explore the important constraints confronted by rural youth while participating in the programmes meant for rural development.

Purao (2000)emphasised over a pivotal strategy to alleviate widespread poverty in rural India. The strategy propounded in this relevant context focused on the active engagement of Community-Based Organizations (CBOs) in the development sector. The research in this regard, underscored the significance of CBOs/VOs as highly effective conduits for reaching impoverished communities. The author argued that to effectively combat poverty, CBOs and Village Organizations (VOs) stand out as the most potent channels. These entities possess a unique vantage point, ideally positioned to identify the genuinely impoverished, discern their specific needs, and recommend tailored programs and interventions to uplift the poor. The manuscript acknowledged that while CBOs may have their limitations and respective shortcomings yet, they remain a formidable and resilient force for reaching marginalized communities. It therefore, emphasised that their enduring strength lies in their ability to bridge gaps, connect with the poorest segments of society, and serve as catalysts for positive change. Thus, despite the above noted certain limitations, Purao's findings resoundingly affirmed the enduring potency of community-based organisations as a formidable means to connect with and support marginalised populations within the society thereby, highlighting the enduring relevance of community-based organisations in the ongoing battle against rural poverty.

Bhasker, Indu and Geethakutty (2001) has analysed the role CBOs in rural development through a case study in Trissure district of Kerala state. Study found that majority of the programmes of the CBOs was Agriculture, health and livelihood specific. It has also revealed that approximately ninety percent of the beneficiaries considered the programmes of CBOs benefited them. Moreover, non-beneficiaries and other stakeholders also considered the works of CBOs are effective for rural development.

Rosemary V. Barnett (2006) conducted a survey with 12 key informants and 418 youth on the development issues contributing to youth involvement, stated that the active collaboration between youth and adults is vital to the long-term success of community development efforts and youth should be empowered to becoming long term contributors to local development efforts. Doing so, youth will be engaged in developing their communities. They will act as a central part of the community development process.

Opare (2007) was of the opinion that though CBOs are small and informal organizations yet they provide various services towards the development of rural communities. However, due to certain weaknesses, CBOs are constraint to provide diverse range of services to their communities. Registrations of CBOs, networking with local to global organizations, leadership development are the indicators upon which attention may be given to strengthen CBOs and improve their service delivery system.

Abegunde(2009) in his study on the role of community-based organizations in economic development in Nigeria: The case of Oshogbo, Osun state, Nigeria found that CBOs are acting as vehicle towards socio-economic development of the community people. CBOs manage their activities on internally generated fund and donations. The study reflected that the contribution of Nigerian government towards promotion of CBOs requires more attention. Active involvement and financial aids from government side is the need to CBOs of Nigeria. Rural Development Report (2019) identified three major foundations for rural youth development: productivity, connectivity and agency. In accordance to the report, improved **connectivity** to people, markets, services, ideas and information create opportunities for rural youth to become more productive. When rural areas have better information and transport links to markets, everyone's opportunities widen, including for rural youth. Greater connectivity also offers them a way to build and strengthen their social and human capital, develop skills and boost their self-confidence. As a result, their **sense of agency** and productivity increase.

YPARD (2020) emphasized that engaging young minds in rural development should be one of the goals of development policies and the strategies to achieve those should be based on the goals. Youth participation in rural development should be improved aiming to help young people build their future in development sector and make them a multi-valued asset. A creative process led by young people need to be followed to increase youth participation which strengthens their ability to participate and lead to sustainable rural development.

According to Vidhyadhar T. Banajawad and Dr.MuktaS.Adi (2021), there have been many aspects like houses, schools and educational institutions, medical and health care facilities, agriculture, industries, nutritional requirements, focusing upon the skill development of the people and facilities such as electricity, energy, water, gas and cooking equipment etc need to be focused upon for rural development which underlines the importance youth engagement in community development. Therefore, the author emphasized to explore the areas like identifying the youth, youth participation & challenges to youth participation. The study made it clear that the role of youth is immense in case of rural development provided they work whole heartedly.

In the well-documented research-based literature by Crossouard, B (2022), the author explores the subject in relevance with regard to the rural youth of south Nigeria. The literature in the given scope of study connotes, that youth of Nigeria have been playing a pivotal role in rural community development of Nigeria. Through the community development programmes many Nigerian youth are trying their best to improve their status. However, maximum number of youth needs to participate actively in community development to achieve objectives like, making youth self reliant through self help projects; ensuring youth's integration for nation building through community development; encouraging youth to cooperate with GOs and NGOs for the fellow youth upliftment and form youth clubs.

Martin P. Mandalu (2023) expressed that the involvement of youth in rural community development initiatives is crucial. In this regard, five core roles of youth have been identified which can contribute to overall development of their communities. These roles are innovators, agents of change, entrepreneurs, advocates, and leaders. Involving youth into CD initiatives; creativity, energy and passion of work towards sustainable development may be tapped in rural areas. It's equally important for the government organizations, civil society organizations and other stakeholders to recognize the importance of youth engagement in rural community development and thus create greater opportunities for the young people to contribute to the development of their communities.

## 2.4 Challenges of Youth Clubs

Langford L. M. Letlhaku (1961) in his research manuscripts postulates the fundamental importance of Youth Clubs in the society. While, advocating through the relevant literature with regard to the indispensable necessity of the youth clubs, the author quite relevant notes for the given context, "Difficulties or problems will not arise in an organization unless the intended objectives are not achieved or the ideals are not achieved in the normal course of management. Therefore, it seems that in order to understand the difficulties of an association, one must first have an idea of the association's goals, objectives, hopes or ideals". The above statement from the journal as noted by the author describes the relevant intricacies of the intimate affairs of any youth club. The inclusion of the above literature review convincingly stands as an important literature to satisfy the scope of the given research.

Plows (2010), in the thought-provoking research article, delves deep into the complex realm of challenging behaviour among youth clubs and young people, a topic of great prominence which has long captured the attention of researchers and even the policymakers. Instead of pigeonholing such behaviour as a mere outcome of individual problems, this study takes a fresh perspective by framing it as a product of social interactions. The focus in the relevant study remains on a youth work environment, particularly on an open-access youth club situated within a Scottish secondary school, where the researchers conducted a year-long ethnographic investigation. The researcher within the scope of such research gets engaged in participant observation, interviews, questionnaires, and review records to unearth compelling insights into the dynamics of challenging interactions in the relevant unique setting. Interestingly, what stands out is the recognition that challenging behaviour serves as an important mechanism for defining the boundaries of acceptable conducts within the youth club's lively and playful atmosphere. Though it remains as both anticipated and normalised, yet it doesn't escape identification and management when necessary. The study emphasises the role of humour and playfulness in navigating and diffusing these challenging interactions. Ultimately, it invites to view challenging behaviour as a social phenomenon that emerges in the moment, offering a richer perspective on working with young people who may be perceived as challenging. It also beckons further research into the emotional dimensions of these interactions, potential differences related to age and gender, and the intriguing relationship between challenging behaviour, creativity, and transformative actions.

Prajapati& Patel (2011) illuminated the formidable challenges faced by rural youth. Among the foremost obstacles identified were the absence of rural youth clubs and their associated activities, limited support from local village institutions, a shortage of effective leadership, and inadequate financial assistance from the government. Notably, the rural youth themselves passionately advocated for a viable solution: the proliferation of rural youth clubs throughout rural regions. Their resounding call echoed the importance of village institutions playing a pivotal role in nurturing these clubs and providing essential training to their members. The youth also underscored the indispensable guidance of local leaders in mentoring and steering these youth clubs toward success. This study underscores the critical significance of fostering collaboration between village institutions, youth clubs, and local leadership, with a particular emphasis on equipping young individuals with entrepreneurial skills. Through this comprehensive approach, rural youth can surmount challenges and embark on a journey toward sustainable growth and self-reliance.

Ayuba A. Aminu (2012) is of the view that there are many problems which disrupts the smooth functioning of youth associations in Nigeria. According to the author fund; basic equipments; below standard projects; scam; honesty issues among the members; political interference are some of the challenges encountered by the youth associations.

In the scholarly work authored by Wattar et al., (2012) the authors embark on a profound Participatory Action Research (PAR) expedition. The manuscript focuses upon unravelling the intricate tapestry of youth perceptions, experiences, and the cultivation of well-being in the remote confines of Paamiut, Greenland. This undertaking unfolds against the backdrop of the community's ardent pursuit of active youth involvement, catalysed by the locally initiated community mobilisation program, PaamiutAsasara. Within the pages of this scholarly narrative, the authors embark on an in-depth exploration of the challenges that pervaded their efforts to encourage youth participation within the PYV initiative. This meticulous examination not only offers a nuanced perspective on the hurdles encountered but also casts a discerning spotlight on the broader implications that surface when the dynamism of youth engagement intersects with the contours of PAR projects. Crucially, the article unfurls a comprehensive methodological tapestry, eloquently detailing the authors' voyage through the research process. This transparent account of their journey elucidates the subtleties inherent in nurturing youth engagement and participation within the PYV project. The scholarly endeavour yields results that are not only thought-provoking but also serve as a poignant reflection of the young populace's intricate understanding and personal encounters concerning their involvement and participation within this unique context.

In 2014, the European Union – Council of Europe youth partnership took a significant step by focusing upon the subject of youth participation. The institutional partnership built the relevant literature upon previous political and research work, which also includes events like symposiums and also conferences. The manuscripts fundamentally deal with several crucial aspects of youth participations in the clubs. The document advocates democratic form of participation in the youth clubs as an important aspect for their functioning. The research-based document comprehensively encapsulates various collective insights garnered from undertaking broad research over previous political and research works. The literature further extends an open invitation to the policymakers, administrators, practitioners, and even researchers to continue championing the cause of youth participation across all facets of young people's lives. Its inclusion within the scope of the current literature review henceforth stands as relevantly appropriate.

Kiilakoski and Kivijärvi, (2015) explores into the multifaceted sphere of Finnish youth clubs, which serve as pivotal arenas for extracurricular learning among the young individuals in the nation. The designated empirical inquiry critically examines such space that is the youth clubs as hubs of non-formal learning, scrutinising the perspectives of both adept youth workers and the youths themselves. The study uncovers an interesting dichotomy, as professional youth workers appear to espouse an educational ideal characterised as the "pedagogy of loose space." This concept posits that educational objectives are most effectively realised when a heterogeneous cohort of young individuals is empowered to autonomously determine their activities under the thoughtful guidance of skilled youth workers. However, as the searchful study delves deeper into the experiences of the youth, a nuanced revelation emerges which reflects that the youth club's intrinsic looseness may not be as self-evident as initially perceived. Instead, an underlying sense of rigidity can inadvertently create barriers, potentially limiting accessibility for various demographic groups. This insightful research thus underscores the imperative for youth workers to pay closer attention to the potentially exclusive spatial practices at play within these educational environments, thereby aligning more harmoniously with the professional aspiration of fostering non-formal learning.

Dolidze (2021) undertakes a valuable study which delves into the enduring hurdles faced by the youth clubs in Georgia. The study offers a glimpse into the real-world challenges that have persisted in the youth clubs over the period of time. It uncovers a diverse range of issues, from the ongoing struggle for the sustainability of youth organisations to the financial constraints that often hamper their operations. Additionally, it highlights the critical importance of addressing human resource challenges and building essential competencies within these clubs. The need for organizational development emerges as a crucial theme, along with the perennial difficulty in securing suitable spaces for their activities. The study also draws attention to the complexities of youth policy implementation, advocating for greater recognition of youth work as a respected profession. Finally, it underscores the imperative of raising public awareness about the youth field and its invaluable contributions to society. This comprehensive exploration offers a roadmap for policymakers, practitioners, and stakeholders seeking to fortify and elevate the youth development landscape in Georgia.

Eriksen and Seland (2021), present a comprehensive exploration of key mechanisms within youth clubs that contribute to the enhancement of well-being among vulnerable young individuals. They propose a novel framework that conceptualizes the prerequisites for youth well-being, emphasizing the significance of providing a secure environment, fostering positive interpersonal relationships, and offering opportunities for personal growth. This conceptual framework transcends conventional psychological perspectives on well-being by incorporating psychosocial theories of youth identity into a sociological context, thereby advancing our understanding of well-being within the dynamic and situated phase of youth. By drawing upon interviews with youth workers and club participants in Norway, the article vividly illustrates how unstructured yet adult-supervised spaces within youth clubs facilitate a sense of safety, belonging, and gradual self-mastery through casual social interactions. The manuscripts delves deep into intrinsic spheres of challenges of youth clubs thereby, mandating its incorporation within the scope of the literature review for this research based manuscript.

A study by Chauke&Malatji, (2021) delves into the formidable challenges confronting professional youth workers in South Africa as they endeavour to deliver crucial youth services. The study responds to a mounting concern within the youth development sector regarding the delayed professionalization of youth work, a situation that exacerbates the vulnerability of these dedicated professionals. Employing a qualitative approach and purposive sampling, the study engaged ten professional youth workers, primarily from non-governmental organisations, with one individual representing the government as a youth officer intern. Data collection involved semi-structured interviews, which were subjected to thematic analysis. The findings resonate with the persistent challenges professional youth workers face in South Africa, including the lack of government recognition, language barriers, salary exploitation, and the demanding nature of their work, often in hazardous environments. The study's salient recommendation underscores the imperative necessity for the National Youth Development Agency to prioritise the professionalization of youth work as a fundamental strategic objective. By doing so, this initiative holds the potential to enhance the quality and impact of youth services across the nation.

The above relevant literature review reveals that community development stands as a meticulously planned process designed to uplift the quality of life for people in both urban and rural settings. This comprehensive approach addresses social, economic, and political aspects to enhance the overall well-being of communities. In the context of rural areas, it encompasses a wide array of strategies and initiatives aimed at improving the welfare and livelihoods of the inhabitants. It emphasizes community organizing and social engagement as pivotal components. Rural development in a country like India holds immense importance, addressing critical needs such as job creation, infrastructure development (including housing, education, and healthcare facilities), agriculture, industry, and essential utilities like electricity, water, gas, and cooking equipment.

Crucially, the involvement of the youth plays a significant role in driving progress in rural areas. Over time, youth engagement in community planning, decision-making, and action has gained traction. Non-profits, volunteer groups, and non-governmental organizations are taking on greater responsibilities in addressing local well-being, underscoring the vital role of youth in these development efforts. Youth groups, in particular, provide a platform for young individuals to channel their talents and energy while actively participating in decisions that impact their communities. Beyond this, participation in such groups fosters valuable skills and values like cultural awareness, respect, responsibility, teamwork, conflict resolution, time management, and communication. These groups contribute to strengthening communities, enhancing engagement in wellness initiatives, recognizing and nurturing talent, building leadership skills, and boosting decision-making and problem-solving abilities. They also help young people develop a positive self-identity and confidence, promote involvement in local governance, and encourage positive peer relationships. However, there are challenges that youth clubs face, including members leaving for education or employment opportunities outside the village, insufficient support from village elders and local officials, a lack of enthusiasm among members, political affiliations within the club, and limited support from village institutions.

In rural areas, apart from agriculture, sectors like infrastructure development, cottage and small-scale industries, and goods processing and marketing are vital for overall economic progress. The literature reveals that youth clubs are often engaged in projects related to agriculture, animal husbandry, poultry farming, and the cultivation of high-yield food varieties for community development. They are typically involved in activities such as sanitation programs, well and tank repairs, library management, afforestation, calf rearing projects, fundraising for community needs, agricultural education, cultural events, and participation in local festivals. Despite their community-focused nature, youth clubs sometimes struggle to effectively influence their communities through their activities. This highlights the need for ongoing efforts to strengthen their impact and engagement within rural areas.

# Chapter – 3

# Research Methodology

The methodology that was used to carry out the study is discussed in detail in this chapter. It details the study's rationale, objectives, research questions, samples, research design, data sources, and tools of data collection.

## 3.1 Statement of the problem

The world is undergoing unprecedentedly rapid change right now. Regardless of geopolitical, socioeconomic, gender, or urban-rural distinctions, the last 50 to 70 years have undoubtedly seen the greatest vicissitudes in all spheres of life. This revolutionary change has a significant impact on our rural communities, particularly on youth.

The lives of young people have been altered by the influence of emerging new media. Globalization makes young people prone to vulnerability. This situation has been further harmed by nuclear families, which have exposed them to individualism, apathy toward sharing one's space in life, a lack of participation in community life, frustration, insecurity, and inability to adapt to change, among other things. These factors to a great extent induced lack of self-confidence, lack of recognition, impatience, mistrust, lack of mutual respect, inability to appreciate others' points of view which in turn added personality and behavioural issues of the youth.

Youth have become victims of circumstances as a result of their psycho-physiological and environmental changes. There are a number of reasons why family and community sharing and mutual cooperation have lost their significance. Although youth has the potential to be a source of energy, society is not reaping the full benefits of its youth because youth as a whole do not find a constructive role to play in the process of social development.

As a result, fostering and guiding young people through deliberate intervention have emerged as a pressing need. Under Nehru Yuva Kendra, youth clubs have been forming to provide a relevant platform for the youth to share their experiences, learn from one another, respect others' points of view, and gain a sense of social belonging, self-confidence, and recognition.

A good number of Youth clubs in Gomati district, Tripura has been participating actively in the activities of community development. At present the state has 1030 registered youth clubs under state cooperative society, Agartala of which 221 are from Gomati district, Tripura. These youth clubs are not free from problems and challenges in implementing programmes. Therefore to make a detailed study on those areas the present problem has been stated like the role of youth clubs in rural community development with special focus on youth clubs of Gomati district, Tripura.

## 3.2 Rationale of the study

Youth clubs mainly focuses on Community base work for the advancement of the local area. Youth clubs primarily engage in voluntary activities for the benefit of their members and the community as a whole. This youth clubs are not able to work properly due to lack of fund and other support from the government and non government organisation in grass rood level. Nehru Yuva Kendra is the main leading organisation to create youth clubs, facilitate youth clubs with trainings, and help in community development process.

With the passage of time NYKs has laid out an organisation of youth clubs in villages and setting up of NYKs have been done there. Youth clubs are organizations based in villages that promote youth empowerment and community development. The purpose of youth clubs is to support the community through developmental projects. Youth clubs use resources from a variety of government departments and other agencies, including national, state, and multilateral institutions, to implement their programs and activities based on local needs.

According to reports, NYK has a network of 2.55 million youth clubs at the village level across India with 50.80 million volunteers from rural youth. It is now the world's largest youth organization. According to the Annual Report of NYK 2020-2021, these Youth Clubs are involved in addressing social issues, community development, and social welfare activities through educational, training, awareness-raising, leadership, and personality development activities (Annual Report of NYK 2020-2021).

The field survey in the Gomati district for the present study revealed that a good number of youth clubs are affiliated under NYK and rendering their services for their community development and it has duly been acknowledged by the key informants of NYK and youth volunteers of the district. But there are also youth clubs which has become non functional due to lack of guidance, facilities, training, fund etc. It is understood during pilot survey that approximately 70 percent of the youth clubs do not have registration, bank passbook, proper records etc. which has been challenging the smooth functioning of the youth clubs and therefore, it becomes an important area of study to ponder over the causes for making youth clubs defunct, problems & challenges and yet to understand the contribution of youth clubs towards community development in Gomati district.

## 3.3 Objectives of the Study

- To understand about the programmes implemented by youth clubs for the community development of the study area.
- To study the problems and challenges encountered by the youth clubs in implementing the programmes in the study area.
- To understand the role of GOs and NGOs for the promotion of the youth clubs in the study area.
- To study the beneficiaries perception about the effectiveness of the programmes conducted by the youth clubs for rural community development.

## 3.4 Research Question

- What are the approaches that youth club adopts for identifying community needs?
- How do the youth club design community development programmes and activities?
- What criteria Government Organisation follows to promote youth clubs?

## 3.5 Universe

The universe comprises of youth clubs of the Gomati District of Tripura. TheGomati district has been selected purposively by the researcher for the present study because of availability ofi) substantial numbers of youth clubsii) Government and NGOs support for promotion of youth clubiii) accessibility through personal acquaintanceiv) research feasibility.For the present study, the researcher selected those youth clubs who were working for rural community development in the Gomati district during the study period (i.e. 2016-2020) and got affiliated under NYK, Tripura before 31st December 2020. As per official information (Nehru Yuva Kendra, Tripura), 189 youth clubs got its affiliation under NYK during the mentioned study period.

## 3.6 Sampling design

The present study adopted multistage sampling method. Firstly, the study identified the eight blocks of Gomati district which are Matabari, Kakrabon, Killa, Tepania, Amarpur, Ompi, Karbook&Silachari. Secondly, functional youth clubs from each block were identified. Thirdly, youth clubs working on rural community development were identified from among the list of functional youth clubs.It is found that out of 189 youth clubs, 132 youth clubs representing eight blocks focusing on rural community development. Fourthly, the beneficiaries of selected 132 youth clubs have been identified which stood around 4751. Fifthly, for smooth conductance of the study 25% of the total youth clubs (132) using lottery method have been selected which constituted 33 youth clubs. Sixthly, to understand the beneficiaries' perception about the effectiveness of the functioning of youth clubs, a proportionate sample of 5% of the total number of beneficiaries for each youth club was selected using random sampling technique which constituted 237 numbers of beneficiaries.

## 3.7 Research Design

The study will be descriptive in nature to obtain accurate and precise information concerning the objectives of the study. The research design is selected to describe in detail the programmes operated by the youth club in rural community development, problems and challenges faced by the youth clubs in implementing the programmes as well as to understand the beneficiaries' perception regarding the implementation of these programmes for rural development. Hence, both qualitative and quantitative methods were employed for the study.

## 3.8 Methods and Tools of Data Collection

The data for this study were gathered using both qualitative and quantitative methods. The primary source of data was collected from the chief functionaries of the youth clubs. For secondary sources of data collection, the researcher consulted previous research works, relevant books, journals, and publications, Government reports, mass media products, web information, websites, etc. The interview schedule as a tool was used for gathering information as per the objectives. The schedule was prepared for the youth clubs, organisations both GOs & NGOs supporting youth clubs for their promotion and for the beneficiaries who received the benefits of the services rendered by the youth clubs.

## 3.9 Data Analysis and Interpretation

Microsoft Excel was used to tabulate and analyze the collected data. Through simple tables and cross tabulations, the quantitative data has been presented. The studies over all findings have been presented in the form of graphs, charts, diagrams, tables.

## 3.10 Limitations of the study

The limitations in respect of conveyance, time and funds which a student researcher would normally encounter were the important limitation to restrict the study to a small area. However, adequate care was taken to make this study as objective, definite and systematic as possible. Moreover, it is a qualitative study based on views expressed by the club members. These views are liable for change over a period of time and additional developments in the area of study. So, the findings of this study cannot be generalized and used in all areas and at all times. However, the findings of this investigation can be generalized to such situations that exist as in the study area. The study is also limited to rural youth clubs those are affiliated under NYK and taking initiatives for rural community development only. Therefore, other youth clubs of urban areas were excluded from the study.

## 3.11 Operational Definition

***Youth:***A social group between the ages of 15-29 according to National Youth Policy 2014.

***Youth Club:*** Community based voluntary organisation promoting youth empowerment and community development.

***Rural:*** The areas other than municipalities and corporations are called rural in the study.

***Community:*** a group of people who share a particular trait or live in the same village.

***Development:*** any effort made to effect positive change. In the study development refers to the youth clubs' initiatives to improve the rural community.

***Rural Community development:*** members of the rural community are made empowered to take collective action for resolving any problem.

***Effectiveness:*** The ability of the youth clubs to create a positive impact over the programmes implemented.

# Chapter – 4

# Study Area: Gomati District, Tripura

The current study has been conducted in the district of Gomati, Tripura. One of the states in the North Eastern Region is Tripura which is surrounded by different other states. On its north, west, south, and south-eastern sides, it borders Bangladesh. Assam and Mizoram are two states in the east that border Tripura on the same side. Agartala serves as the state's capital which got its status as a separate state by the Indian Union on January 21, 1972.

**Map of Tripura Containing all Districts**

## 4.1 Tripura State – At a Glance

**4.1.1 Administrative Division:** Tripura covers 10,491,69 square Km., with eight districts, including the West Tripura, Sepahijala, Khowai, South Tripura, North Tripura, Unakoti, Dhalai and Gomati District. It has one autonomous district council, twenty three sub-divisions with 58 blocks, 45 revenue circles and 222 Tehsils with 897 revenue moujas.

**4.1.2 Population:** According to the 2011 census, 36, 73,917 people are living in the State. Among which 18, 74,376 are male and 17, 99,541 female (Census of India 2011).

**Total Population of the State**

| Sl. No | Description | Total Population |
|---|---|---|
| 1. | Total Population | 36,73,917 |
| 2. | Male Population | 18,74,376 |
| 3. | Female Population | 17,99,541 |
| 4. | Rural Population | 27,12,464 |
| 5. | Urban Population | 9,61,453 |

Source: Census of India 2011

**4.1.3 Population by Religion:** According to the 2011 census, 3,063,903 people are living in the State are Hindu which is the largest. And the second largest group comprises of 3, 16,042 population are Muslim. (Census of India 2011)

**Population by Religion**

| Sl. No | Religion | Population |
|---|---|---|
| 1. | Hindu | 3063903 |
| 2. | Muslim | 316042 |
| 3. | Christians | 159882 |
| 4. | Buddhists | 125385 |
| 5. | Sikhs | 1070 |
| 6. | Jains | 860 |
| 7. | Others | 1514 |

Source: Census of India 2011

**4.1.4 Literacy Rate:** According to the 2011 census, overall literacy rate of the state is 87.2 percent (Census of India 2011)

### Literacy rate of the State

| Sl. No | Description | Literacy Rate (%) |
|---|---|---|
| 1. | Overall literacy rate | 87.2 |
| 2. | Male literacy rate | 91.5 |
| 3. | Female literacy rate | 82.7 |
| 4. | Scheduled tribe literacy rate | 79.05 |
| 5. | Scheduled Caste literacy rate | 89.45 |

Source: Census of India 2011

## 4.2 Gomati District-At a Glance

In 2012, the Gomati District with its headquarters in Udaipur was established. The District is bounded on the north by the Dhalai district and the West Tripura District and the other sides are surrounded by Bangladesh, an international border. Udaipur is known as the "city of lakes" and served as the capital of Tripura until 1760 A.D. Gomati district covers 2,966 square kilometres and approximately 25% of the state's total land area. The Mata Tripura Sundari Temple, which is about 3 km away from Udaipur at Matabari, made the city renowned.

### 4.2.1 Administrative Structure

| Sl. No. | Parameters | Particulars |
|---|---|---|
| 1. | Sub-division | 3 nos (Amarpur, Karbook, Udaipur, ) |
| 2. | Block | 8 nos (Matabari, Kakrabon, Killa, Tepania, Amarpur, Ompi, Karbook & Silachari) |
| 3. | Municipal Council | Udaipur Municipal Council |
| 4. | Nagar Panchayat | Amarpur |
| 5. | Revenue Village | 132 |
| 6. | Gram Panchayat | 70 Nos |
| 7. | ADC Villages | 95 Nos |
| 8. | Habitations | 1158 Nos. |

Source: Census of India 2011

### 4.2.2 District Population

| Sl.No. | Parameters | Particulars |
|---|---|---|
| 1. | Total Population | 4.41,538 |
| 2. | Male | 2,25,428 |
| 3. | Female | 2,16,110 |
| 4. | SC Population (No. and % of total population) | 74,430: 16.85% |
| 5. | ST Population (No. and % of total population) | 1,88,554: 42.70% |
| 6. | Total Geographical area | 139311 |

Source: Census of India 2011

### 4.2.3 Literacy Rate of the District

| SL.No | Parameters | Particulars |
|---|---|---|
| 1. | Overall literacy rate | 84.50% |
| 2. | Male literacy rate | 89.94% |
| 3. | Female literacy rate | 78.90% |

Source: Census of India 2011

### 4.2.4 Cooperative Societies

| SL. No | Parameters | Particulars |
|---|---|---|
| 1. | Total Number of Societies with members | Society – 89, Members-58,083 |
| 2. | SHG with total members | 5182 (SHG), 58515 (Members) DRDA. |
| 3. | Women SHG with total members | 3055 (SHG), 31794 (Members) DRDA. |
| 4. | ST Women SHG with total members | 3105 (SHG), 13686 (Members) DRDA. |
| 5. | SC Women SHG with total members | 654 (SHG), 6289 (Members) DRDA. |

Source: Census of India 2011

## 4.3 Youth Population in the State & District

According to 2011 Census, the total population of Youth in the age group of 15-29 years is 2.53 lakh out of which 1.27 lakhs male and 1.25 lakh females. A total of 29.12 percent of the district's population is made up of young people between the ages of 15 and 29 (2011 census of India).

## 4.4 Genesis of Youth Club in Gomati District

Nehru Yuva Kendra, Udaipur was established on January 21, 1986, in Udaipur, Tripura, under the supervision of Mr. Chakraborty, Nandadulal. The objective of the Kendra was to focus youth non students of rural area for inculcating in them the values associated with nationalism and channelize their effort and participation in different development drives at the grassroots level in the district.

NYK Udaipur looks after the youth clubs of Gomati district and South Tripura District of Tripura. A total of 333 youth clubs from both the districts were registered till date. Of which a total of 221 youth clubs and MahilaMandals belongs to Gomati District. Out of which 189 youth clubs of Gomati district were affiliated to NYK.

# Chapter – 5

# Presentation & Discussion of Findings

The present chapter provides information about the findings of the study conducted on Youth clubs in Rural Community Development: A study in Gomati District, Tripura. Information has been collected on different variables from the 33 youth clubs affiliated under NYK and working in Gomati districts and from the beneficiaries which has helped the researcher to analyze and interpret the responses accordingly.

The first objective of the study was to understand the programmes implemented by youth clubs for the community development in Gomati District. The study was conducted on 33 youth clubs from the Gomati districts of Tripura. The interview schedule for the said objective has been divided into eight sections:i) Profile of the youth club;ii) Profile of the youth club members;iii) Accounts & record keeping;iv) Preparation of Action plan; v) About the programmes; vi) Coordination with line departments; vii) Funding process; viii) Reporting & monitoring.

The second objective was to study the problems and challenges encountered by the youth clubs in implementing the programmes. The interview schedule had sections on i) Implementation of the programme; ii) Problems & challenges encountered with different sub heads like a) Staff members; b) Community mobilisation; c) Coordination & Cooperation; d) Financial aspect; e) Monitoring & Evaluation.

To understand the role of GOs and NGOs for the promotion of youth clubs in the study area was the third objective of the study which had subsections on i) profile of the organisation ii) about the programme iii) role of GOs for youth club promotion iv) role of NGOs for youth club promotion.

The fourth and the last objective of the study were to understand beneficiaries' perception about the effectiveness of the programmes conducted by the youth clubs for rural community development in the study area. The interview schedule for this objective has been formulated with sections on i) profile of the beneficiary ii) awareness about youth club iii) perception about effectiveness of the services. The responses have been collected under each head and presented through graphs, charts, and tables.

## 5.1 Profile of the Youth Club

**5.1.1 Profile of the Youth Club:** The thirty three youth clubs of Gomati district, Tripura were studied for the present study. To gain an understanding on the first objective i.e. to understand the programmes implemented by the youth clubs, initially the profile of the youth clubs were collected. All select youth clubs were affiliated with Nehru Yuva Kendra (NYK). The table below depicts the profile of youth clubs includes block wise youth club; year of establishment, registration & affiliation of youth clubs.

There are eight rural development blocks in Gomati District. Youth clubs were selected from each of these blocks, details of which are provided below:

**Table 5.1: Block wise Youth Clubs**

| Sl.No | Name of the block | Name of the Youth Club | Address |
|---|---|---|---|
| 1. | Tepania R D Block | i.Aranyak Club | Karaimura, Tepania |
| | | ii. Jewel Club | Dhajanagar |
| | | iii. Gomati SamajikSanghtha | Hadra |
| 2. | Ampi R D Block | i. NabaudoiSangha | AmpiBazar,Ampi |
| | | ii. Baishyamani Para sports club | Baishamanipara |
| | | iii. Budhu Sadhu memorial Club | Taidu |
| | | iv. Teenmurty club | Shantipur |
| 3. | Kakraban | i. RRPC | Kishoreganj |
| | | ii. Evergreen club | Tulamura |
| | | iii. Brain Power Youth Society | Jamjuri |
| 4. | Killa | i. Boys student club | Keipengbulai |
| | | ii. Samai Club | Kwaimura |
| | | iii. Salka Club | Tentuibari |
| | | iv. Kwthar Club | Harekami |
| 5. | Matabari R D Block | i. Dharmangkur Youth Society | Tainani |
| | | ii. Achin Baba Sangha | Gorjee |
| | | iii. Satadal play Centre | East Bagabassa |
| | | iv. TarunSangha | Kusharghat |
| | | v. JatiaYuvaSanghstha | Rajnagar |
| | | vi. Reformist Society | Bhangarpar |
| | | vii. New star club | Haripur |
| | | viii. TarunSangha | Matabari |
| | | ix. Renessaiance Club | Kunjaban |
| | | x. Netaji Welfare Centre | Maharani |

| 6. | Silachari R D Block | i. DejayJodha Club | Silachari |
|---|---|---|---|
| | | ii. Club Wasna | Jayantapara |
| | | iii. Swamiji Welfare Society | Silachari |
| 7. | Amarpur R D Block | i. Swamiji social welfare society | Sripur |
| | | ii. Vivekananda club | Amarpur |
| | | iii. Red star club | Amarpur |
| | | iv. Nabashakti club | Natunnagar |
| 8. | Korbook R D Block | i. Eleven star club | Jatanbari |
| | | ii. Tiger sound club | North Ektachari |

The details of 33 youth club's about their establishment, registration and affiliation are presented below:

**Table 5.2: Year of Establishment, Registration & Affiliation**

| Sl. No | Name of the Youth Club | Established | Year of Registration | Year of Affiliation under NYK | Registered under |
|---|---|---|---|---|---|
| 1. | Aranyak Club | 2004 | 2013 | 2016 | Cooperative Society, SangeetkalaAcademy,West Bengal, ICAT,State YA & Sports |
| 2 | Jewel Club | 1984 | 1991 | 2016 | YA & Sports, Sangeetkala Academy West Bengal, Education, ICAT |
| 3 | Gomati SamajikSanghtha | 2000 | 2007 | 2016 | ICAT, YA & Sports |
| 4 | NabaudoiSangha | 2009 | NA | 2017 | NA |
| 5 | Baishyamani Para sports club | 1983 | 1992 | 2016 | YA&Sports,ICAT, TSA |
| 6 | Budhu Sadhu memorial Club | 2005 | NA | 2016 | NA |
| 7 | Teenmurty club | 2001 | NA | 2017 | NA |
| 8 | RRPC | 1987 | 1996 | 2018 | YA& Sports |
| 9 | Evergreen club | 1992 | 2006 | 2016 | ICAT, YA & Sports, NABARD, Agriculture |
| 10 | Brain Power Youth Society | 2011 | 2015 | 2019 | CEC, YA & Sports, KIDZEE |
| 11 | Boys student club | 2004 | 2009 | 2016 | YA & Sports |
| 12 | Samai Club | 1992 | 1997 | 2016 | YA & Sports |

...

| | | | | | |
|---|---|---|---|---|---|
| 13 | Salka Club | 1996 | 2003 | 2016 | ICAT, YA & Sports |
| 14 | Kwthar Club | 2002 | NA | 2017 | NA |
| 15 | Dharmangkur Youth Society | 2013 | 2017 | 2016 | YA&Sports,ICAT, SDM,NABARD |
| 16 | Achin Baba Sangha | 1996 | 2002 | 2016 | NABARD, Red cross, ICAT,Sangeetkala Academy, West Bengal, CEC, SDM |
| 17 | Satadal play Centre | 2001 | 2011 | 2018 | |
| 18 | TarunSangha (Kusharghat) | 1986 | 1992 | 2016 | NABARD,ICAT,Red cross |
| 19 | JatiaYuvaSanghstha | 1997 | 2001 | 2016 | ICAT, YA & Sports, |
| 20 | Reformist Society | 2014 | 2018 | 2017 | SangetkalaAcademy,WestBengal,ICAT,NABARD, Kathaksociety of India, New Delhi, YA & Sports |
| 21 | New star club | 1989 | NA | 2016 | NA |
| 22 | TarunSangha (Matabari) | 2005 | 2012 | 2018 | YA& Sports |
| 23 | Renessaiance Club | 1998 | 2007 | 2017 | SDM, YA & Sports, |
| 24 | Netaji Welfare Centre | 2001 | 2009 | 2018 | NABARD |
| 25 | DejayJodha Club | 1998 | NA | 2017 | NA |
| 26 | Club Wasna | 2007 | NA | 2018 | NA |
| 27 | Swamiji Welfare Society | 2006 | NA | 2018 | NA |
| 28 | Swamiji social welfare society | 2001 | NA | 2017 | NA |
| 29 | Vivekananda club | 2001 | NA | 2017 | YA & Sports |
| 30 | Red star club | 1999 | 2008 | 2017 | ICAT, YA & Sports |
| 31 | Nabashakti club | 2008 | NA | 2019 | YA & Sports |
| 32 | Eleven star club | 1991 | 1995 | 2016 | ICAT, YA & Sports |
| 33 | Tiger sound club | 2011 | NA | 2016 | NA |

The above table 5.2 depicts that the old groups took more than ten years to register and another ten years to become connected with NYK. The following figuresshow how the explanation is properly justified.

**5.1.2 Year of Establishment of Youth Clubs:** The study included all youth clubs affiliated under NYK during the study period (2016-2020) and worked in the Gomati district for rural community development. Under this backdrop it was interesting to know about the year of establishment as a youth club so as to understand their progress of work. The below chart shows the year wise establishment of the youth clubs selected for the study. They were grouped into four groups having 10 yrs span of time (Chart 5.1).

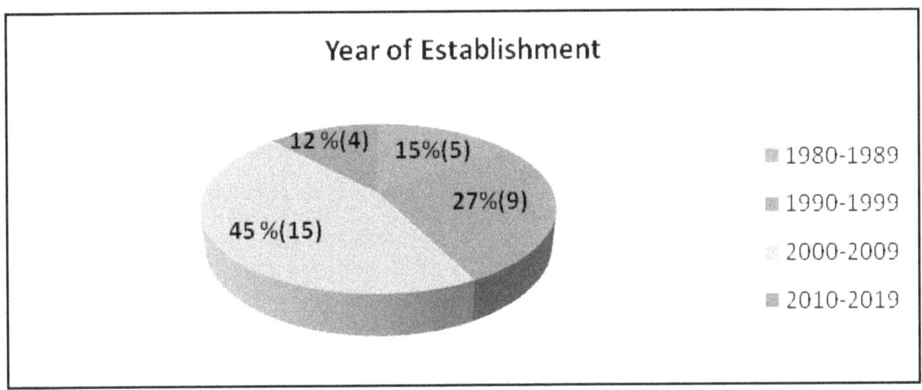


**Chart 5.1: Year of Establishment**

Chart 5.1 outlines that 45 percent youth clubs were established in between 2000-2009 followed by 27 percent during 1990-1999 and 15 percent between1980-1989 & 12 percent youth clubs established during 2010-2019. According to the findings, youth clubs have been operating in the Gomati district since the 1980s, and their number gradually increased from 2000 to 2009. It also reflected the fact that only four youth clubs were established in the last ten years—from 2010 to 2019—because the majority of youth were already engaged with youth clubs for the past forty years.

**5.1.3 Year of Establishment Vs Year of Registration:**Youth Club is a place where young people in a particular area can meet, talk, and plan activities for the development of themselves and the community. Registration in youth clubs earns public and government trust. Youth clubs that are registered are more dependable in the eyes of the general public and governments. Consequently, the study placed an emphasis on understanding the clubs' registration status. The study found that 36.36 percent (12 clubs) are not registered and that 63.64% (21 clubs) are registered. The time frame between the establishment and registration of selected youth clubs were grouped into three groups like 0–5 years, 6–10 years, and 11–15 years.

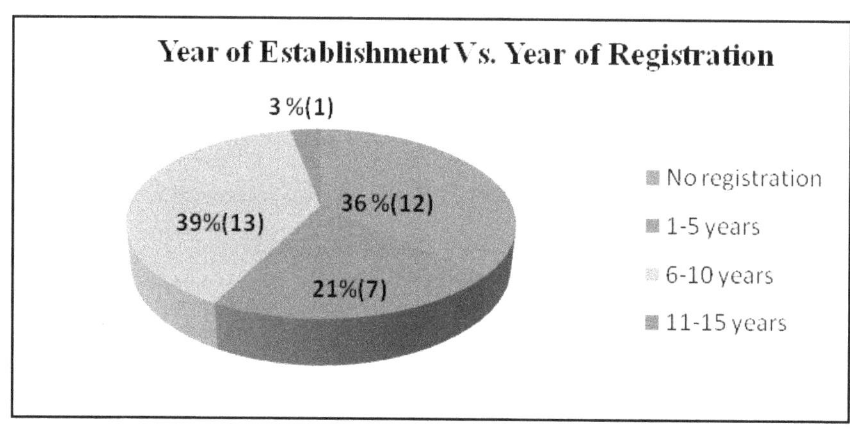


**Chart 5.2: Year of Establishment Vs Year of Registration**

The statistical data presented in chart 5.2 shows that there is disparity between the year of establishment and the length of time it took to register under Cooperative societies, NABARD etc. The study found that a maximum of 39 percent youth club has taken 6 to 10 years of time for registration followed by 21 percent took 1 to 5 years and 3 percent took 11 to 15 years. Despite the fact that clubs were established and started operating in the study area since 1980s, yet in majority cases it took almost 10 years to feel the need of a registration for formalising their operations.

**5.1.4 Target Population:** Youth clubs cater to a diverse range of people. They have been working not only for the youth but also for the community's most vulnerable members, including women, children, the elderly, and the disabled, among other groups. The youth clubs have chosen their target population based on the club's scope and mission (Table 5.3).

**Table 5.3: Target Population of the Youth Club**

| Target Population | No.of Clubs | Percentage |
|---|---|---|
| Youth | 33 | 100.00 |
| Women | 29 | 87 |
| Children | 17 | 51 |
| Elderly | 7 | 21 |
| Substance Abuse | 4 | 12 |
| Disability | 5 | 15 |

According to Table 5.3, the youth clubs are also focusing on the growth of women, children, the elderly, and so on. It implies youth clubs are managing more than one category of beneficiaries. The findings indicate that 87 percent of youth clubs target both youth and women, with 100% putting an emphasis on youth development. 51 percent of youth clubs are implementing child welfare initiatives, followed by 21 percent for elderly people and

15 percent for people with disabilities. The remaining 12 percent are concerned with substance abusers and 6 percent are involved in community development as a whole.

**5.1.5 Sources of Fund:** The 33 youth clubs were studied to know the sources of fund for different activities. The responses highlighted that there are more than one source of fund for each organizations. It was also studied that the organizations get fund either through self generation or from line department. The self generated funds are mainly membership Fees, Government funding and donation along with some other activity specific fund raising. In addition to the line departments listed below, NYK, RSETI, BDO, and Panchayat are the primary line departments that donate funds to the clubs. The results of the responses are presented in table 5.4 for each organization.

**Table 5.4: Funding Source of the youth clubs**

| Sl. No | Name of the Youth Club | Source of Fund: Self generated | Source of fund from Line department |
|---|---|---|---|
| 1. | Aranyak Club | Self-generated, Donation,Central and state govt., Rent House, Fishery, Plantation of bananas etc | NYK, Agriculture, BDO, RSETI, Health, |
| 2 | Jewel Club | Self generated membership fees, Community fund drive, Donation, Rent House, MLA Dev. Fund, Government funds(states), Training Centre (Computer, Bamboo and cane product) | NYK, Health, SBM, Block, DA, Social welfare, RSETI, CEC, Bamboo Mission |
| 3 | Gomati SamajikSanghtha | Self generated membership fees, Community fund drive, Donation, Award, Central and state govt. programme, Decorator, Art School | NYK, BDO,SBM, Panchayat |
| 4 | NabaudoiSangha | Self generated membership fees, Donation, Central and state govt., | NYK, BDO, SBM, RSETI |
| 5 | Baishyamani Para sports club | Self generated membership free, Decorator and sound system, Donation, Community fund drive, Sports tournaments, Computer education centre | Youth Affairs & Sports, MLA dev. fund, SBM, ADC |
| 6 | Budhu Sadhu memorial Club | Self generated membership fees, central /state govt. agencies, Donation, Community fund drive, Fishery | NYK, Block, ADC |
| 7 | Teenmurty club | Self generated membership fees, Community fund drive, Donation, Kid Zee school, ART and Dance school | NYK, ADC, SBM |

...

| | | | |
|---|---|---|---|
| 8 | RRPC | Self generated membership fees, Donation, Central and state govt. programmes | NYK, SBM |
| 9 | Evergreen club | Self generated membership fees, Community fund drive, Donation, Fishery, Central and state govt. schemes, Fishery, Agar Plantation, Couching centre for Class IX and X | NYK, Agriculture, Forest, SBM |
| 10 | Brain Power Youth Society | Self generated membership fees, Community fund drive, Donation | NYK, CSR |
| 11 | Boys student club | Self generated membership fees, Donation, central and state govt. programme, Sponsorship | NYK, ADC, Youth Affairs & Sports, MLA dev. Fund, ICAT |
| 12 | Samai Club | Self generated membership fees, Central and state govt.scheme, Donation, Rubber plantation, Fishery, Can and craft Training centre and product selling | NYK, ADC, ICAT,MLA dev. Fund, RSETI, Agriculture, Fishery,NABARD, Rubber Board |
| 13 | Salka Club | Self generated membership fees, Community fund drive, Donation, central and state govt. programme | NYK |
| 14 | Kwthar Club | Self generated membership fees, Community fund drive, Donation, state and central govt. programme | NYK |
| 15 | Dharmangkur Youth Society | Self Generated membership fees, Donation, Decorator, Projector rent, Fishery, Bana Plantation, small Brick industry and flower plantation, central and state govt programmes, SHG, Small scale Industry, SHG, NABARD, | NABARD, NYK, Agriculture, Fishery, KVIV, SDO, ADC, RSETI, SSI, Co-operative society. |
| 16 | Achin Baba Sangha | Self generated membership fees, Central and Stategovt. programme, Rent House, Decorator, CEC, Fishery, NABARD, SHG, Awards, JFMS, Achin baba dargah, Donation, Skill development training centre, Internet Café and Typing, Mini ATM | NYK, NABARD, RESETI, BDO, Agriculture, Fishery, SBI bank,SDM,SBM, Panchayat |
| 17 | Satadal play Centre | Self generated membership fees, Central/State govt. agencies, Donation, School, ART and dance school, Battlenut and coconut, Fishery | NYK, ICAT, Agriculture, Fishery |

| | | | |
|---|---|---|---|
| 18 | TarunSangha (Kusharghat) | Self generated membership fees, Central state govt. programme,Donation, Rent House, Decorator, Sound system, Cultural instrument rent, | NYK, Block, Panchayat |
| 19 | JatiaYuvaSanghstha | Self generated membership fees, Community fund drive, Donation, Rent House | NYK, Panchayat, BDO |
| 20 | Reformist Society | Self generated membership fees, Community fund drive, Donation, Sponsorship, Dance school, ART school, Small scale industry, public Lottery, Cultural programme, Sponsorship etc | NYK, ICAT |
| 21 | New star club | Self generated membership fees, Community fund drive, Donation | NYK |
| 22 | TarunSangha (Matabari) | Self generated membership fees, Community fund drive, Donation | NYK |
| 23 | Renessaiance Club | Self generated membership fees, Donation, Central and state govt. programmes, House rent, Art and Dance class, Skill development training Centre and computer education centre, printing, xerox and stationary shop, SHG | NYK, SDM, Tata Thrust, Health, SBM, RSETI, Panchayat |
| 24 | Netaji Welfare Centre | Self generated membership fees, Donation, Central and state govt., School, Art and dance class, Fishery, Battlenut, Coconut etc. | NYK, YA & Sports, BDO, RSETI, Health, Agriculture, Education |
| 25 | DejayJodha Club | Self generated membership fees, Donation, central and state govt. programme, Coaching centre for football, Art School | Youth Affairs & Sports, NYk, MLA dev. Fund, ADC, SBM |
| 26 | Club Wasna | Self generated membership fees, central and state, Donation, Community fund drive | NYK, ADC, SBM, Health, Social welfare |
| 27 | Swamiji Welfare Society | Self generated membership fees, Community fund drive, Donation, Yoga Training centre, Decorator, Sound system | NYK |
| 28 | Swamiji social welfare society | Self generated membership fees, Donation, Central and state govt. programmes, Fishery and Coaching centre for Class IX to XII, SHG | NYK |

...

| | | | |
|---|---|---|---|
| 29 | Vivekananda club | Self generated membership fees, Community fund drive, Donation, Sponsorship, Yoga centre, Couching centre for Class VIII to XII, Central and state govt. programmes, CSR funds | YA & Sports, NYK, Palatana power project(CSR) |
| 30 | Red star club | Self generated membership fees, Rent House,Fishery, SHG, Auto Stand, Donation | NYK |
| 31 | Nabashakti club | Self generated membership fees, Community fund drive, Donation, Sports tournament, Art school, | NYK |
| 32 | Eleven star club | Self generated membership fees, Central and Stategovt. programme, Rent House, Decorator, CEC, Fishery, Donation, Skill development training centre | NYK, Block, ADC |
| 33 | Tiger sound club | Self generated membership fees, Community fund drive, Donation | NYK |

**5.1.6 Area of coverage:** During the data collection process, it was discovered that many youth clubs operate in a variety of villages within distinct blocks and reach a significant number of people through their programs. The information pertaining to the area of the youth clubs being studied is presented in the table below.

**Table 5.5: Area of coverage of the youth clubs**

| Sl. No | Name of the Youth Club | No. of Village | No. of Blocks | Population |
|---|---|---|---|---|
| 1. | Aranyak Club | 4 | 4 | 772 |
| 2 | Jewel Club | 1 | 2 | 1086 |
| 3 | Gomati SamajikSanghtha | 1 | 2 | 404 |
| 4 | NabaudoiSangha | 2 | 2 | 439 |
| 5 | Baishyamani Para sports club | 1 | 1 | 478 |
| 6 | Budhu Sadhu memorial Club | 1 | 2 | 213 |
| 7 | Teenmurty club | 2 | 1 | 429 |
| 8 | RRPC | 2 | 2 | 487 |
| 9 | Evergreen club | 2 | 2 | 483 |
| 10 | Brain Power Youth Society | 1 | 1 | 287 |
| 11 | Boys student club | 2 | 1 | 343 |
| 12 | Samai Club | 4 | 1 | 972 |
| 13 | Salka Club | 1 | 1 | 389 |

| | | | | |
|---|---|---|---|---|
| 14 | Kwthar Club | 1 | 1 | 311 |
| 15 | Dharmangkur Youth Society | 3 | 2 | 477 |
| 16 | Achin Baba Sangha | 4 | 4 | 877 |
| 17 | Satadal play Centre | 2 | 2 | 478 |
| 18 | TarunSangha (Kusharghat) | 1 | 1 | 431 |
| 19 | JatiaYuvaSanghstha | 1 | 2 | 366 |
| 20 | Reformist Society | 3 | 2 | 843 |
| 21 | New star club | 1 | 1 | 286 |
| 22 | TarunSangha (Matabari) | 2 | 1 | 367 |
| 23 | Renessaiance Club | 3 | 2 | 632 |
| 24 | Netaji Welfare Centre | 2 | 3 | 519 |
| 25 | DejayJodha Club | 2 | 1 | 354 |
| 26 | Club Wasna | 1 | 1 | 276 |
| 27 | Swamiji Welfare Society | 2 | 3 | 577 |
| 28 | Swamiji social welfare society | 2 | 3 | 544 |
| 29 | Vivekananda club | 2 | 2 | 493 |
| 30 | Red star club | 2 | 1 | 491 |
| 31 | Nabashakti club | 2 | 2 | 657 |
| 32 | Eleven star club | 3 | 2 | 523 |
| 33 | Tiger sound club | 1 | 2 | 356 |

Out of 33 youth clubs, eight cover more than two villages and blocks, as shown in Table 5.5. The findings reflected that out of 8 clubs, 4 clubs (Achin baba, Aranyak, Samai&Jwel) have been working in 4 villages of 4 development blocks and 4 clubs (Dharmangkur, Eleven Star, Reformist Society, Renaissance club) have been working in 3 villages of 2 blocks. Other youth clubs are also operating in 1 or 2 villages of 1 or 2 blocks. The data indicates that clubs are functioning well. It is also a fact that these organizations have been in the community development work since 1980s.

## 5.2 Number of Members in Youth Club

A youth club's members are important because they carry out the organization's mission and have influence over people in the community. A youth club's success or failure is determined by the types and number of members it has. The number of members associated to carry out the activities in each youth club is depicted in the below chart 5.3.

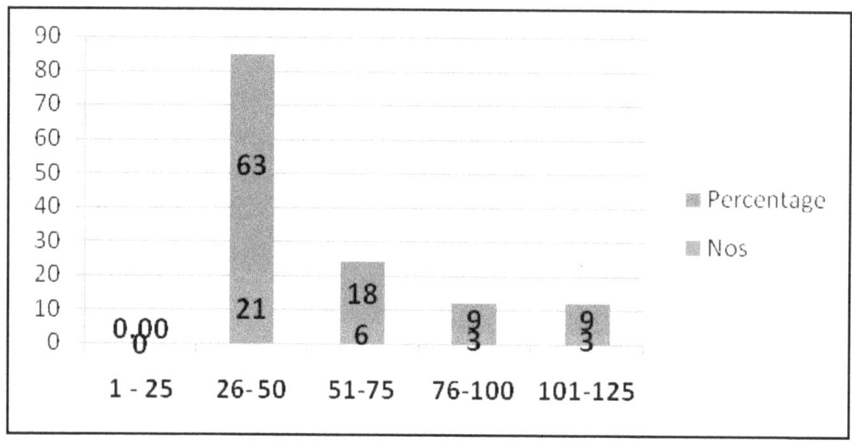


**Chart 5.3: Members in Youth Club**

Chart 5.3, shows that out of 33 youth clubs, 21 (63 percent) youth club has members between 26 to 50, and 6 (18 percent) has 51 to 75 members. 3 (9 percent) youth club has 76 to 100 members and 101 to 125 members only a 3 youth club has. The data make it clear that the majority of the clubs have 26 to 50 members.

**5.2.1 Age of the Club Members:** As per National youth policy 2014, an individual between the age group of 16-25 will be called a youth and they can form a youth club for their all-round development. Against this backdrop, the researcher found it relevant to understand the age composition of the club members. Therefore, they were grouped into six age groups: 15-19 years, 20-24 years, 25-29 years, 30-35 years, 36-45, and above 46 years of age. The chart below depicts the respondents' age groups.

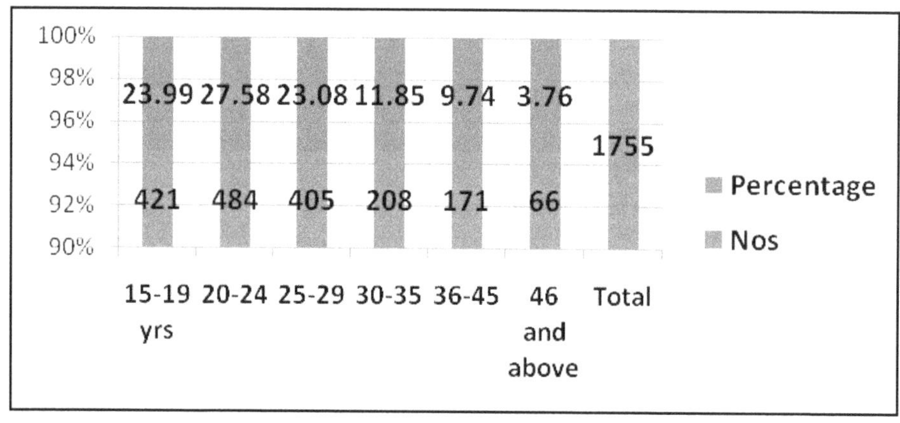


**Chart 5.4: Age of the Club Members**

Chart 5.4, presented above shows that out of 1755 members of 33 youth clubs, 27.58 percent (484) members are in the age group of 20-24 years, followed by 23.99 percent (421) from the ages of 15-19 years & 23.08 percent (405) are in the ages of 25-29 years. Around

11.85 percent (208) of the members are from 30-35 years and about 9.74 percent (171) are between the ages of 36-45 years & 3.76 percent (66) members are from above 46 years of age. This indicates that most of the members of the club are within the age group of 20-24 who are young and energetic.

**5.2.2 Gender of the Club Members:** The study also aimed to determine gender-specific participation in club activities. The gender-specific participation in club activities for community development is depicted in chart 5.5.

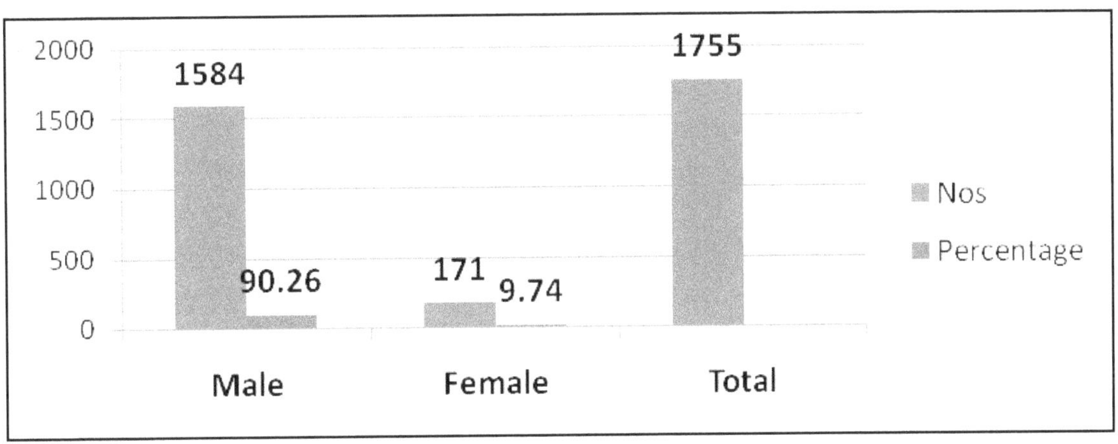


**Chart 5.5: Gender of the Club Members**

According to chart 5.5, 90.26 percent (1584) of the 1755 people who belong to all 33 clubs are men, while only 9.74 percent (171) are women. In the Gomati district of Tripura, this demonstrates that men are more involved in club activities than women are.

**5.2.3 Occupation of the Members:** The social status of human being to a great extent is determined by their occupation. Good occupation gives humans higher distinction in their families and general public. Therefore, it has drawn an interest in the researcher to find out the occupational status of the members and to understand the reason behind becoming a member of a youth club which does not have any scope for earning. Thus, the information related to the occupational background has been collected and presented in chart 5.6.

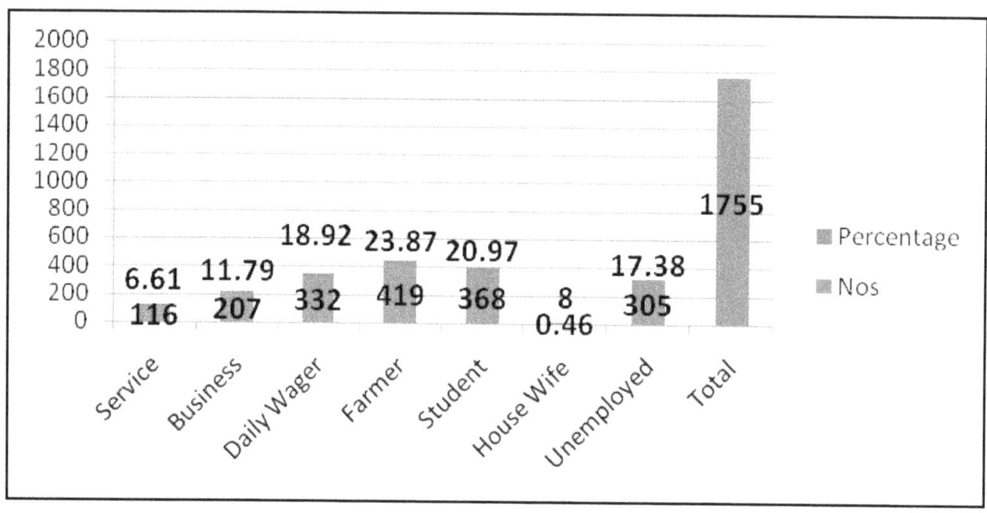


**Chart 5.6: Occupation of the Club Members**

Out of 1755 members of 33 youth clubs, 23.87 percent are farmers who rely on farming for their livelihood, while 20.97 percent are students, as shown in Chart 5.6. 18.92 percent members are daily wagers and 11.79 percent members are engaged with some sort of business. About 6.61 percent of the members are employed, while 17.38 percent is unemployed. The data make it clear that cultivators make up the majority of youth club members, followed by students.

**5.2.4 Category wise Members in youth club:** It has been observed that youth clubs have members of almost every category, regardless of gender or religion, to participate in developmental activities. It also opens up opportunities to learn about gender representation in clubs by category. As a result, table 5.6 contains comprehensive information about each youth club organized by category.

**Table 5.6: Membership profile of the youth clubs**

| SL No | Name of Youth Club | Total member of Youth club | Male | Female | General(UR) | SC | ST | OBC | Minority |
|---|---|---|---|---|---|---|---|---|---|
| 1. | Aranyak Club | 39 | 37 | 2 | 14 | 16 | 4 | 5 | 0 |
| 2. | Jewel Club | 81 | 75 | 6 | 23 | 19 | 11 | 16 | 12 |
| 3. | Gomati samajikSanghtha | 56 | 52 | 4 | 17 | 14 | 0 | 16 | 9 |
| 4. | NabaudoiSangha | 55 | 51 | 4 | 17 | 13 | 0 | 17 | 8 |

| | | | | | | | | | |
|---|---|---|---|---|---|---|---|---|---|
| 5. | Baishyamani Para sports club | 72 | 66 | 6 | 0 | 0 | 72 | 0 | 0 |
| 6. | Budhu Sadhu memorial Club | 31 | 31 | 0 | 0 | 0 | 31 | 0 | 0 |
| 7. | Teenmurty club | 35 | 33 | 2 | 8 | 11 | 9 | 7 | 0 |
| 8. | RRPC | 31 | 30 | 1 | 13 | 11 | 0 | 7 | 0 |
| 9. | Evergreen club | 53 | 47 | 6 | 13 | 22 | 8 | 11 | 0 |
| 10. | Brain Power Youth Society | 27 | 25 | 2 | 5 | 16 | 0 | 5 | 0 |
| 11. | Boys student club | 106 | 92 | 14 | 0 | 0 | 106 | 0 | 0 |
| 12. | Samai Club | 49 | 46 | 3 | 0 | 0 | 49 | 0 | 0 |
| 13. | Salka Club | 43 | 38 | 5 | 0 | 0 | 43 | 0 | 0 |
| 14. | Kwthar Club | 38 | 32 | 6 | 0 | 0 | 38 | 0 | 0 |
| 15. | Dharmangkur Youth Society | 127 | 91 | 36 | 3 | 5 | 103 | 5 | 11 |
| 16. | Achin Baba Sangha | 117 | 87 | 30 | 26 | 33 | 22 | 25 | 11 |
| 17. | Satadal play Centre | 56 | 53 | 3 | 19 | 11 | 0 | 16 | 10 |
| 18. | TarunSangha | 42 | 40 | 2 | 17 | 13 | 0 | 9 | 3 |
| 19. | JatiaYuvaSanghstha | 46 | 42 | 4 | 9 | 17 | 0 | 13 | 7 |
| 20. | Reformist Society | 102 | 87 | 15 | 25 | 37 | 0 | 31 | 9 |
| 21. | New star club | 26 | 26 | 0 | 7 | 5 | 0 | 9 | 7 |
| 22. | TarunSangha | 39 | 39 | 0 | 0 | 0 | 39 | 0 | 0 |
| 23. | Renessaiance Club | 87 | 79 | 8 | 27 | 34 | 13 | 9 | 4 |
| 24. | Netaji Welfare Centre | 36 | 36 | 0 | 19 | 13 | 0 | 4 | 0 |
| 25. | DejayJodha Club | 35 | 32 | 3 | 0 | 0 | 35 | 0 | 0 |
| 26. | Club Wasna | 29 | 29 | 0 | 0 | 0 | 29 | 0 | 0 |
| 27. | Swamiji Welfare Society | 37 | 37 | 0 | 12 | 17 | 0 | 6 | 1 |
| 28. | Swamiji social welfare society | 27 | 25 | 2 | 3 | 11 | 8 | 4 | 1 |
| 29. | vivekananda club | 35 | 35 | 0 | 7 | 13 | 9 | 6 | 0 |
| 30. | Red star club | 49 | 44 | 5 | 13 | 19 | 0 | 17 | 0 |
| 31. | Nabashakti club | 41 | 41 | 0 | 0 | 0 | 41 | 0 | 0 |
| 32. | Eleven star club | 69 | 67 | 2 | 13 | 22 | 14 | 13 | 7 |
| 33. | Tiger sound club | 39 | 39 | 0 | 7 | 14 | 6 | 7 | 5 |
| | **TOTAL** | **1755** | **1584** | **171** | **317** | **386** | **690** | **258** | **105** |

## 5.3 Bank Accounts & Maintenance of Accounts

**5.3.1 Bank Accounts:** A bank account may keep an organisation legally compliant, provide some financial security and help the organisation to appear more professional to the stakeholders. Therefore, the study intended to know about the bank account status of the selected youth clubs. The findings are presented in chart 5.7.

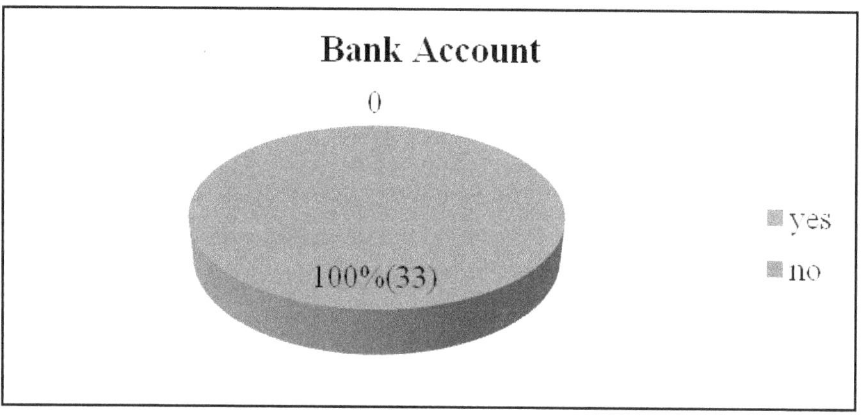


**Chart 5.7: Bank Accounts of Youth Clubs**

In order to keep track of financial transactions, all 33 youth clubs (100 percent) selected for the study have bank accounts with various banks, as shown in Chart 5.7. There are no such instances of clubs lacking bank accounts.

**5.3.2 Audit of Accounts:** The audit of account is also important as it provides credibility to a set of financial statements and gives the shareholders confidence that the accounts are true and fair. It can also help to improve an organizations internal account control mechanisms. This has further paved a scope to know about the audit status of the youth clubs. Information in this regard has been collected and presented in chart 5.8

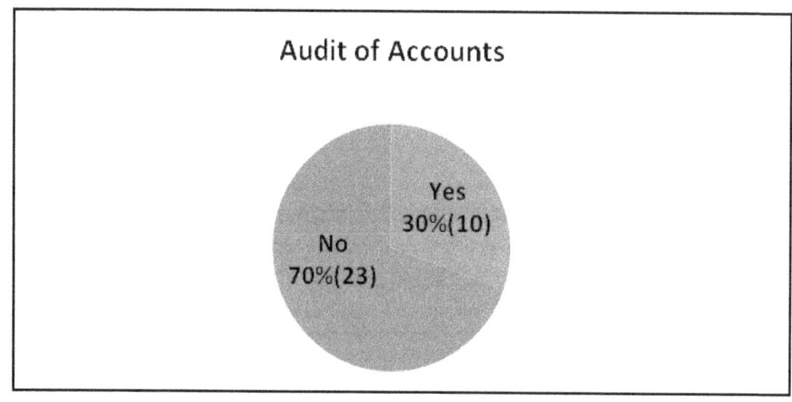


**Chart 5.8: Audit of Accounts of Youth Clubs**

According to Chart 5.8, despite the fact that all select youth clubs have bank accounts for financial transactions, only 30% (10) of them have audited accounts, and 70% have no audited accounts.

**5.3.3 Record Keeping:**Record keeping is essential for the proficient activity of any organisation. Proper record keeping becomes very helpful when reviewing and monitoring a club's performance. Therefore, the study investigated the club member's attitude towards record keeping. Information in this regard has been collected and presented through chart 5.9.

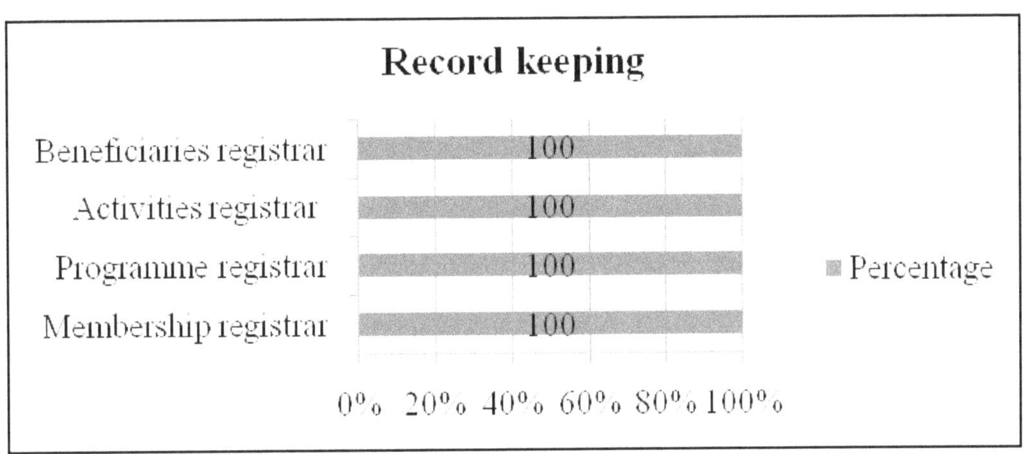


**Chart 5.9: Record Keeping of Youth Clubs**

The chart 5.9 shows that the all youth clubs affiliated under NYK are properly maintaining their records in the form of different registers like beneficiaries' registrar; activity registrar; programme registrar, membership registrar.

**5.3.4 Action plan and Activity report:**Making an action plan and activity report for an organisation is important as it enlists the steps to be taken to achieve a specific goal. The action plan breaks down the goal into actionable steps that can easily be followed and tracked. Activity report keeps staff informed about the past, present and future tasks. Keeping in view the importance of action plan and activity report, the study investigated the stand of youth clubs in this regard (Table 5.7).

**Table 5.7: Action Plan & Activity Report**

| Response | Preparation of Action Plan | Preparation of Activity Report |
|---|---|---|
| **Yes** | 33 (100%) | 19 (58%) |
| **No** | 0 | 14 (42%) |
| TOTAL | 33 (100%) | 33 (100%) |

Table 5.7 shows that (100 percent) of the 33 youth clubs have prepared an action plan. Among these, 58% of youth clubs have produced activity reports. The reason for this is that youth clubs are required to develop an action plan for obtaining funding during affiliation and in order to receive funding from the government. As a result, every youth club creates an action plan when they request funding as a required document. However there are instances for not preparing activity report by 42% of the youth clubs.

## 5.4 Programmes of the Youth Clubs

All the programmes of youth clubs either directly benefit the youth for their own individual growth or the communities. Youth clubs normally come up with need – based programmes and raise the funds necessary to run them. Both Government and Non Government Organisations are supporting youth clubs by making a part of programme implementation. A detailed presentation of the programmes has been given in table 5.8.

**Table 5.8: Community development Programs of the youth clubs**

| Sl. No | Programme | Budget | Duration of the programme | Beneficiaries |
|---|---|---|---|---|
| 1. | Skill development Training Programme | 20000 | 2 month | women, Girls, Widow |
| 2. | Awareness programme on Cancer and Screening | 2000 | 1 day | Community |
| 3. | Skill development Training on Broom making, Paper bag making | 16000 | 7 days | Community |
| 4. | Training on EDP | 8000 | 2 days | Youth Clubs Members, small Businessman owner, Women Group, SHGs |
| 5. | Awareness programme on FashalBimaYojana, Soil Health card schemes | 3000 | 1 day | Farmers from local area |
| 6. | Awareness programme on swacha Bharat Mission (SBM) like organising Rally, Miking, IEC distribution, Open defecation Free Block, Street play in Market, Schools, Door to Door campaign | 30000 | 1 month | Community |
| 7. | 1000 sample plantation programme | 25000 | 1 month | Community |

| | | | | |
|---|---|---|---|---|
| 8. | Training on Youth Leadership and Community development programme(TYLCD) | 88000 | 5days | youth, club members, mahilamandals |
| 9. | Tree plantation and Distribution, | 4500 | 1 day | Community |
| 10. | Training on EDP | 4000 | 1 day | SHG, Youth, Business owner, Community |
| 11. | Prayas programme for mass awareness on importance of police & Different types of crimes. | 3000 | 1 day | Community |
| 12. | Awareness programme on HIV/ AIDS | 8000 | 1 day | Community |
| 13. | Skill Development Training | 30000 | 2 months | Women |
| 14. | Awareness programme on Schemes of KVIB | 4000 | 1 day | Community |
| 15. | SBM awareness programme | 30000 | 1 month | Community |
| 16. | Fish Feeds and Seeds support Programme and Training to farmers for culture of fish in scientific line | 3000 | 1 day | Community, Fishery owner |
| 17. | Awareness programme for farmers on different schemes of Agriculture department | 500 | 1 day | Farmers of local area |
| 18. | Awareness programme on SHG and Microfinance, different programme under Tata Trust Agartala | 3000 | 1 day | Community |
| 19. | Awareness on Disaster Management and DRR, First Aids Training | **No Budget sanction but expenditure borned by NGO** | 1 day | Community |
| 20. | Block level Youth Parliament | 12000 | 1 day | Community |
| 21. | Skill development Training on Bamboo and Cane product | 30000 | 2 month | Women |
| 22. | Cancer screening camp and Awareness programme | 5000 | 1 day | Community |
| 23. | Awareness programme on Substance abuse | 3000 | 1 day | Community, Youth, Student |
| 24. | Awareness programme on dairy Farming and Animal Husbandry | 6000 | 4 days | Community |

...

| | | | | |
|---|---|---|---|---|
| 25. | Awareness on Income Generating Activities | 3000 | 1 day | Youth, Community |
| 26. | Awareness on Environment and Climate Change | 4000 | 1 day | Community |
| 27. | Mega Health Check Up camp | 15000 | 1 day | Community |
| 28. | Awareness on Environment and Climate Change | 4000 | 1 day | Community |

**5.4.1 Sources of Fund for programme implementation:** What gives visibility or recognition to any clubs or organisation is their work and activity towards community development. Out of the 33 respondents some are running program by themselves or some are running projects planned by govt. and also some donor agencies. Some clubs are having more than one source. The funding nature of the program of the respondents Youth Clubs are as follows in chart 5.10

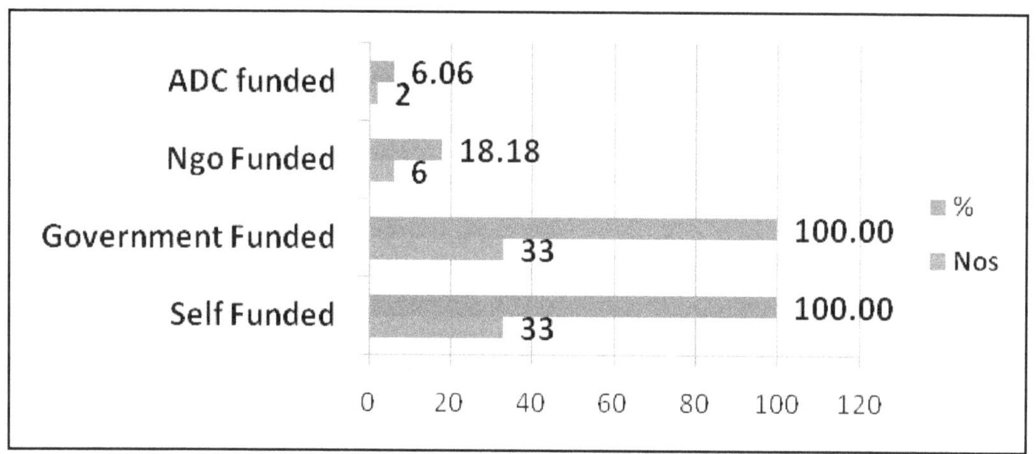


**Chart 5.10: Sources of Fund for Youth Clubs**

Chart 5.10 explains that 100% (33) of the youth clubs are both self funded and also are running on Govt. fund. Among them there are 18.18% (6) youth clubs who have also been funded by NGOs on different projects and 6.06% (2) of the youth clubs are funded by ADC.

**5.4.2 Community Development Programme Implemented:**The previous discussion has made it clear that the youth club runs programs for both community and personal growth. Since the study is about the growth of rural communities, more thought has been given to this issue. Table 5.9 shows the number of programs that were implemented with the help of NYK, an autonomous organization run by the Government of India, NGOs, self-funded programs, and donations from other sources.

**Table 5.9: Programs implemented during study period**

| Sl. No. | Name of Youth Club | NYK supported program | Other org. supported program | Self funded programs | Programs conducted after raising fund from external sources |
|---|---|---|---|---|---|
| 1. | Aranyak Club | 9 | 5 | 6 | 1 |
| 2. | Jewel Club | 10 | 6 | 11 | 3 |
| 3. | Gomati samajikSanghtha | 6 | 2 | 5 | 1 |
| 4. | NabaudoiSangha | 10 | 7 | 5 | 1 |
| 5. | Baishyamani Para sports club | 4 | 4 | 7 | 2 |
| 6. | Budhu Sadhu memorial Club | 4 | 0 | 6 | 0 |
| 7. | Teenmurty club | 4 | 1 | 2 | 0 |
| 8. | RRPC | 5 | 3 | 8 | 0 |
| 9. | Evergreen club | 7 | 2 | 5 | 1 |
| 10. | Brain Power Youth Society | 5 | 4 | 8 | 2 |
| 11. | Boys student club | 8 | 6 | 9 | 2 |
| 12. | Samai Club | 9 | 3 | 13 | 0 |
| 13. | Salka Club | 6 | 1 | 5 | 0 |
| 14. | Kwthar Club | 4 | 2 | 7 | 0 |
| 15. | Dharmangkur Youth Society | 11 | 13 | 17 | 5 |
| 16. | Achin Baba Sangha | 11 | 13 | 21 | 4 |
| 17. | Satadal play Centre | 3 | 2 | 7 | 0 |
| 18. | TarunSangha | 9 | 4 | 11 | 2 |
| 19. | JatiaYuvaSanghstha | 10 | 4 | 9 | 1 |
| 20. | Reformist Society | 9 | 5 | 12 | 3 |
| 21. | New star club | 5 | 1 | 7 | 0 |
| 22. | TarunSangha | 5 | 2 | 7 | 0 |
| 23. | Renessaiance Club | 9 | 2 | 11 | 3 |
| 24. | Netaji Welfare Centre | 4 | 2 | 7 | 0 |
| 25. | DejayJodha Club | 5 | 1 | 7 | 0 |
| 26. | Club Wasna | 4 | 0 | 2 | 0 |
| 27. | Swamiji Welfare Society | 6 | 1 | 4 | 0 |
| 28. | Swamiji social welfare society | 4 | 0 | 2 | 0 |
| 29. | Vivekananda club | 3 | 1 | 6 | 0 |

| 30. | Red star club | 5 | 2 | 9 | 1 |
|---|---|---|---|---|---|
| 31. | Nabashakti club | 3 | 1 | 5 | 0 |
| 32. | Eleven star club | 4 | 2 | 6 | 1 |
| 33. | Tiger sound club | 4 | 0 | 2 | 0 |
| | TOTAL | 205 | 102 | 249 | 33 (205+102+249+33=589) |

The summary of the table is highlighted in chart 5.11 below

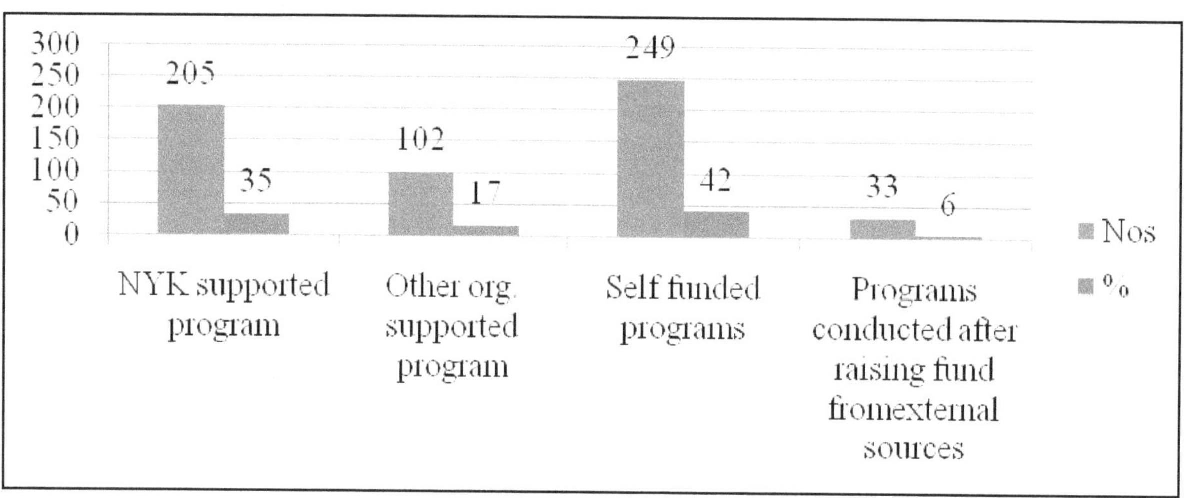


**Chart 5.11: Supported Community Development Programmes**

According to Chart 5.11, all 33 youth clubs put on a total of 589 community development programs between 2016 and 2020. The majority of the programs 42 percent were self-funded. Nehru Yuva Kendra (NYK) supported the next highest number of programs, which was 205, with 35 percent of the total. 17% (102) of the programs were supported by other organizations, and 6% (33) of the programs were organised with the raised money through things like donations, lotteries, competition entry fees, etc.

## 5.5 Procedure for acquiring NYK sponsored programmes

A youth club first needs to get affiliated under NYK and then apply for programs. The steps are explained below:

***Step 1:*** A properly constituted Youth Club may submit an affiliation application to the NYK office together with the Memorandum of Association, Bye-laws, proceedings of the General Body meeting, and a list of members. The NYKS website offers an online approach for youth clubs to affiliate themselves, or they can download an application form and submit it offline to the relevant District NYK.

***Step 2:***The NYK may grant affiliation certification and a special number to the Youth Club after verifying all required documentation.

***Step 3:***Within seven days of submitting the online Affiliation Form, the Youth Club will be associated with the district Nehru Yuva Kendra if it is already registered under the Societies Registration Act, 1860, or any State Act with a similar purpose.

***Step 4:*** If the youth club is not registered as described above, the district Nehru Yuva Kendra will physically check it out. If the youth club meets the requirements, it will be connected with the district NYK within 30 days after submitting the online Affiliation Form.

***Step 5:*** The user name and password will be issued to the applicant Youth Club via email at the address specified in the address data as soon as the District Youth Coordinator affiliates the Youth Club. The Youth Club can log in by clicking "Already Registered; Login" using this User Name and Password. The Youth Club can print the letterhead for the club, visiting cards for individual members, and affiliation certificates after successfully logging in.

***Step 6:*** The Youth Club would be able to engage, partner with, and utilise the services offered by NYKS after affiliation. Once a Youth Club joins NYK, the range of programming accessible to them expands, and they can take part in all of the activities that NYK sponsors.

The youth clubs have faced a numerous problems while implementing the programmes. The problems have been studied in terms of Staff strength, Motivation for community service, Skill for community mobilization; Coordination & Cooperation with line departments, Financial matter etc. A detailed statistical presentation on each category has been made in the following charts for developing a comprehensive understanding on the problems.

## 5.6 Problems faced by the Youth Clubs

**5.6.1 Staff strength:** In order to achieve an organization's goals, efficient employees are crucial. In addition, ensuring availability of sufficient staff to complete day to day task is also important. Being short-staffed can increase the work pressure and potentially may affect the process of organizational growth. Therefore, the study intended to investigate the staffing situation of youth clubs whose results are presented in chart 5.12.

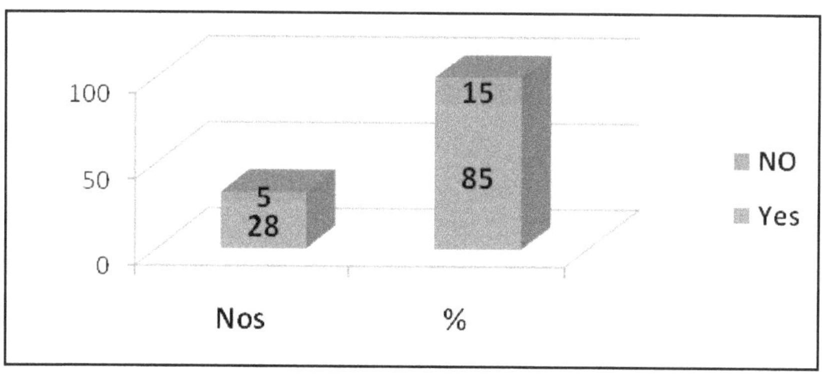


**Chart 5.12: Staff Strength of Youth Clubs**

As indicated by Chart 5.12, out of 33 youth clubs 85percent (28) youth clubs communicated that they have no problem with staff. They have adequate staff to run their programmes while 15% (5) youth clubs are understaffed for which they face difficulties to implement the programmes at the community level.

**5.6.2 Role performance by Staff:** It has been observed that the organization achieves success when staff members carry out their assigned roles or responsibilities with utmost sincerity and dedication. When roles are played well, trust grows and everyone feels better and more engaged. In the absence of this, employees are more likely to feel disconnected from their work, which may have an impact on the organization's operation. The researcher conducted an investigation into the role performance of the staff in accordance with their assigned responsibilities with this background information, and the results are presented in chart 5.13.

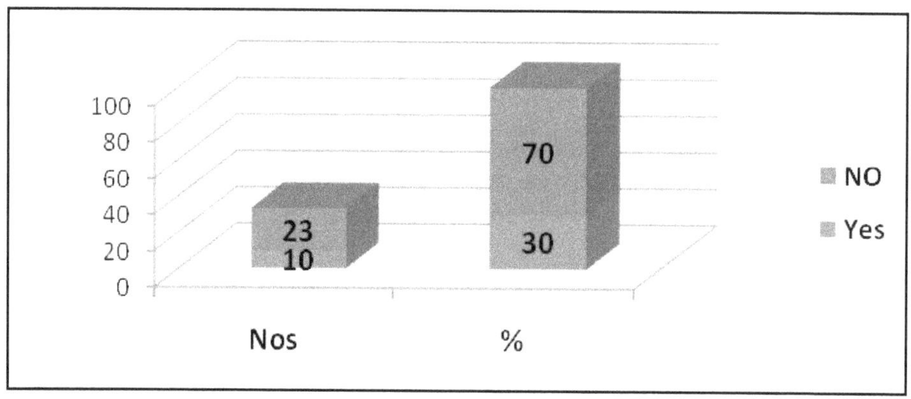


**Chart 5.13: Role Performances by Staff of Youth Clubs**

According to Chart 5.13, staff members at 70 percent of youth clubs do not take their responsibilities seriously, while only 30% (10) fulfil their assigned roles. As a result, it is thought that most clubs have staff, but they aren't doing their jobs well.

**5.6.3 Motivation for community service:** It is assumed that members, who are willing to understand more about their community and interested to learn about community work, are motivated for community service. They also feel that their services will develop their community and the community will be self-sustained. Therefore, the study intended to investigate the motivation level of club members toward community services. Findings concerning the above are presented in Chart 5.14.

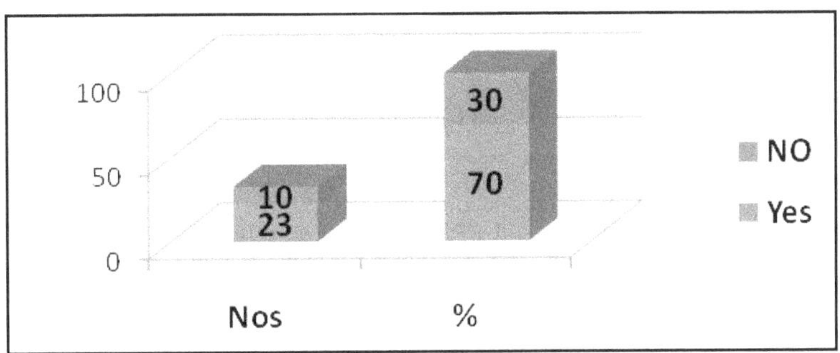


**Chart 5.14: Youth Club's Motivation for Community Service**

According to chart 5.14, 70% (23) of members are not exclusively committed to community service, whereas 30% (10%) are. According to the findings, 70% of people who do not want to work in community service are primarily victims of poverty due to under-employment and thus would work for a community with minimum wages.

**5.6.4 Mobilisation of Resources:** Resource mobilization is essential for an organisation to take it at the next level by meeting all needs of the staff, community and society at broader context. The organisation should have understanding on the resources like knowledge, money, media, labour, internal & external support from power elite. Organisation should also know about management process and communication pattern that can contribute for organizational development and relationship building for higher resource mobilization. Information collected in this regard from the select organisation is presented in Chart 5.15.

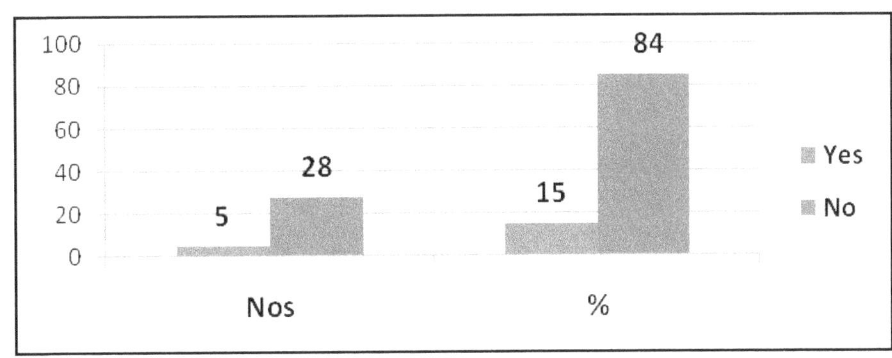


**Chart 5.15: Resource Mobilization by Youth Clubs**

The data presented in above chart 5.15, indicates that 15 percent of the youth clubs can mobilize their resources, whereas 84 percent of clubs are dependent on their partner organization for resource mobilization. The findings highlighted the importance of providing adequate knowledge to the youth clubs on resource mobilization so as to respond to community issues immediately with their available resources.

**5.6.5 Community support:** The primary factors that determine a club's success or failure in terms of programs are the community's' response and participation. The study focused on finding out whether the community is supportive or not with regards to the initiatives undertaken by the youth clubs for community development and the findings in this regard are presented in chart 5.16.

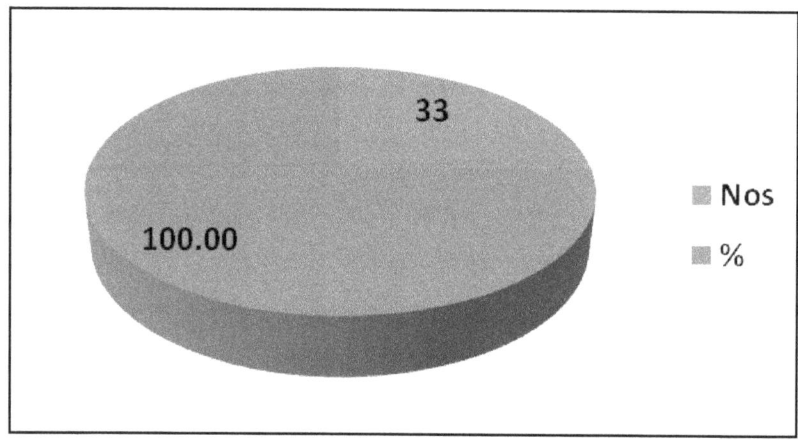


**Chart 5.16: Community Support Received by Youth Clubs**

Chart 5.16 shows that 100 percent of the community people are supporting and co-operating the club activities, and this is the sole reason for the existence of these clubs.The data indicates that the club members are dedicated to developmental activities and a great extent motivated too. But to ensure their 100 percent motivation and dedication, necessary steps have to be taken up by the Government and NGO youth organizations.

**5.6.6 Cooperation of the members:** The success of any program depends on the efficiency of its members. If the members are not skilled or are not supported, it brings a setback to the program. The clubs do not have employees and are mostly run by members and hence the cooperation of the members in sharing the responsibilities of the programs is very important. The study focused on the cooperation received from the internal club members and the findings are explained below in chart 5.17

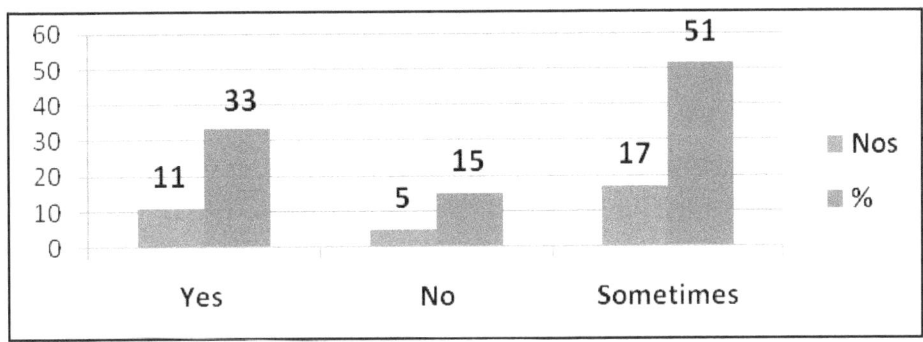


**Chart 5.17: Cooperation among the members of Youth Clubs**

The Chart 5.17, depicts that 51 percent of the members extend their hands of cooperation sometimes as per their availability of time and convenience. It is found that 33 percent of the total members are always there with full cooperation for successful implementation of the programmes and it is observed that members of governing body make up majority of these groups. It is also found that 15 percent members are not cooperating, which may be because members are volunteers and not employees.

**5.6.7 Cooperation of the partner organisation:** Every club that works with a partner organization relies on their partners for important things like funding, monitoring, reporting, and other things. The clubs' ability to run the program is harmed if the partner organizations are not responsive or cooperative. The study tried to understand the nature of cooperation received from the partner organization and the finding are explained below in Chart 5.18.

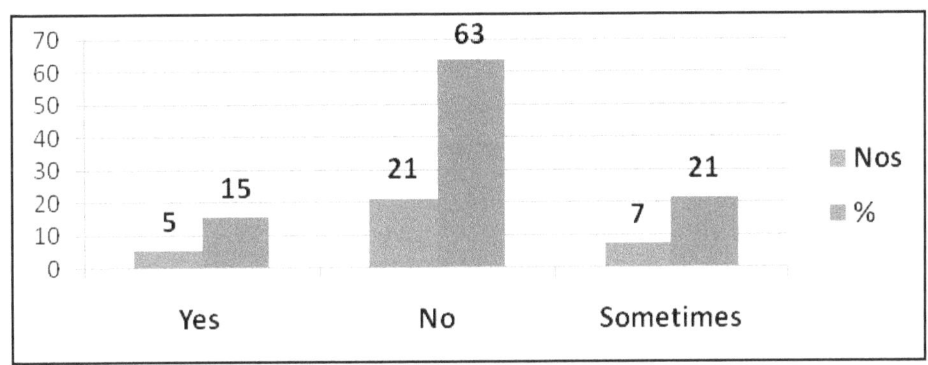


**Chart 5.18: Cooperation received from the Partner Organisation**

According to Chart 5.18, 21 percent of organizations have stated that they occasionally receive support, but 63 percent (21 of the organizations) have stated that they do not receive timely support from partner organizations. Just 15 % (5) of the organisation expressed to have gotten full help from partner organisation.

**5.6.8 Fund receiving status:** Fund is an essential component for running an organisation, particularly for implementing programmes. It is observed in different studies that organizations partnering with other funding agencies sanction fund timely but takes time in releasing. As a result, As a result, it becomes extremely challenging for a small organization like youth clubs to make significant financial management decisions for a project. Such instances gave a scope to the study to collect information in this regard and accordingly presented in chart 5.19.

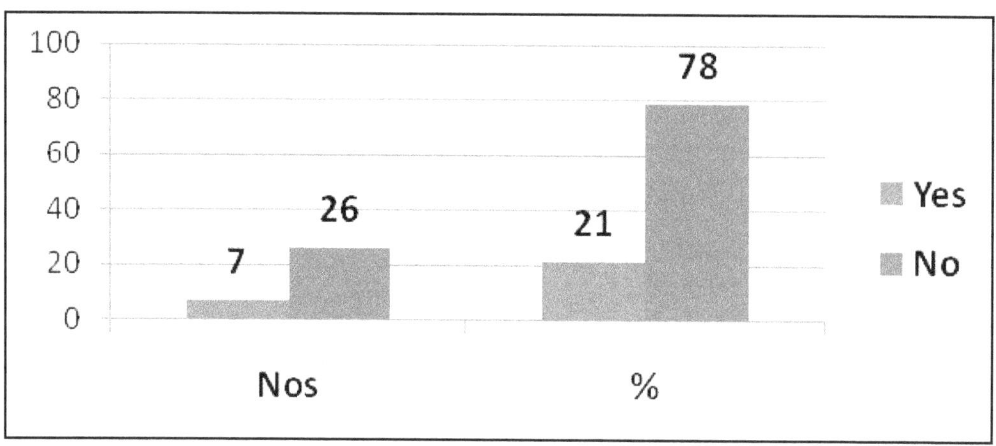


**Chart 5.19: Fund received from Funding Agencies**

The above Chart 5.19, indicated that 26 percent of the youth clubs stated that the funding agencies release funds on time while 78.79 percent of clubs stated that funds are not released on time. Irregular funding becomes a barrier to the clubs' development efforts when they are working for the benefit of the community. In addition to that, all 33 youth clubs expressed that the fund allocated for a programme is also not sufficient to address the needs of a larger community group. Moreover, funds are released after the programme. Therefore, to continue with the programme, the youth club again has to generate funds from different sources.

**5.6.9 Cooperation from funding agencies:**People from various professions and backgrounds can collaborate to solve important problems by exchanging ideas, sharing information, and working together in cooperation. Additionally, cooperation addresses the requirements for interaction, responsibility sharing, and communication between and among various agencies. Therefore, it was pertinent for the study to determine whether or not the youth clubs have received cooperation from external and funding agencies prior to, during, and after the program's implementation. On this, information has been gathered and presented in chart 5.20.

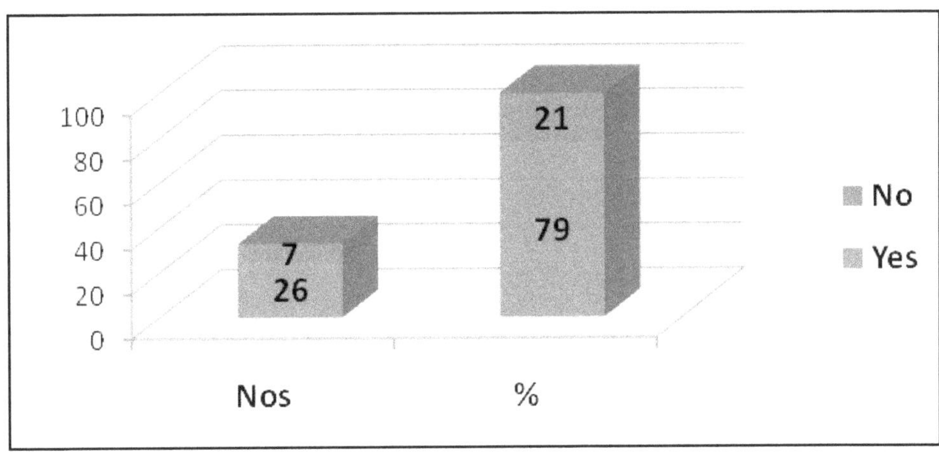


**Chart 5.20: Cooperation from Funding Agencies**

According to the information on cooperation that is presented in Chart 5.20, 79 percent of youth clubs agreed that the funding agency, such as NYK, responds very promptly to the queries raised by youth clubs and extends cooperation for resolving the issue. In any case, 26 percent of the respondents are of the view that funding agencies are either delayed to answer or don't like to answer by any means during need.

**5.6.10 Monitoring Process:** Monitoring of the work is again very essential for a youth club to make their progress effective. Monitoring helps organizations identify potential issues, track progress, and measure outcomes. This also helps the organization formulate need-based strategies and identify the areas of improvement which meet the organization's goals and objectives. Understanding the importance of monitoring, the study tried to explore any problem associated with it. Information has been collected on this and presented in chart 5.21.

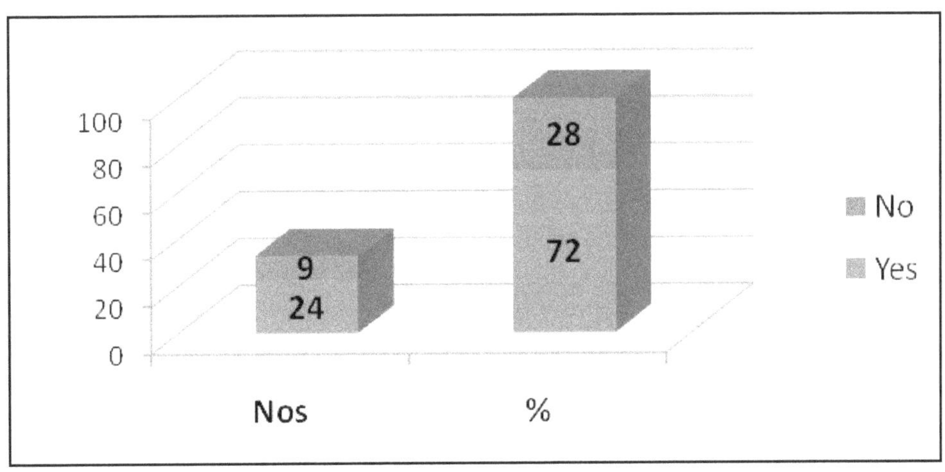


**Chart 5.21: Monitoring Process by the Funding Agencies**

According to chart 5.21, 72 percent of the youth clubs viewed that funding agencies are monitoring the progress of the work whereas 28 percent youth clubs are of the opinion that funding agencies are not monitoring the progress as per scheduled time which hinders the progress of the work.

Further, the youth clubs were asked to answer whether the feedback after monitoring is shared with the youth clubs or not and the responses collected are presented below in chart 5.22

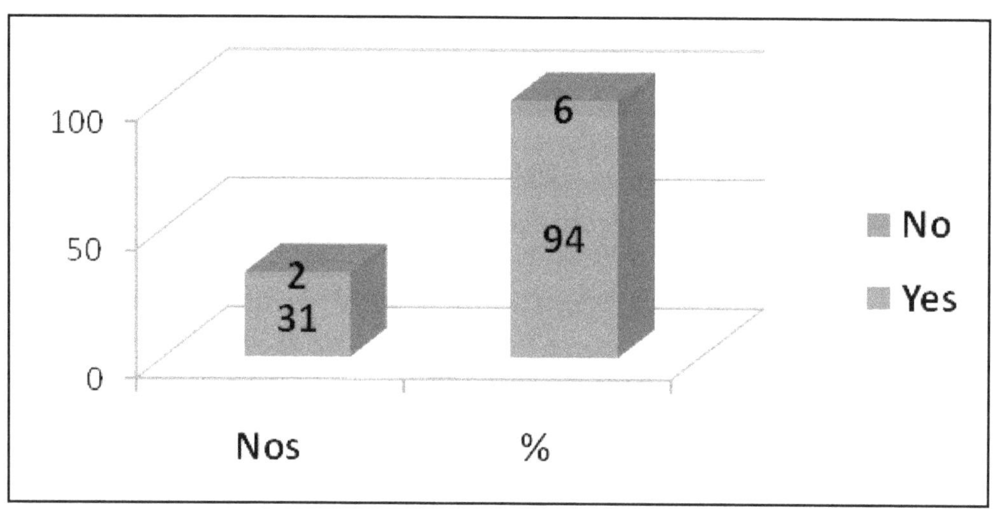


**Chart 5.22: Feedback sharing by funding agency after monitoring**

The above Chart 5.22 depicts that 94% (31) of the youth clubs stated that they received feedback from the funding agency after monitoring by them where as 6% (2) of the youth clubs expressed that they do not receive any feedback from the funding agency after their monitoring process is done.

## 5.7 Challenges of youth Club

The study found that some challenges are being faced by the youth clubs. Therefore, the respondents were approached to share the challenges faced by them. It is found that youth clubs are confronting various difficulties and these are combined and explained below through a diagram 5.1

## Diagram 5.1.:Challenges of youth Club

a. **Financial Issues**: The majority of youth clubs have had trouble securing sufficient and ongoing funds to carry out their activities. Obtaining donors is a difficult undertaking, and occasionally Clubs may face significant difficulties in dealing with the fundraising requirements of a particular donor. Additionally, they have a lot of trouble obtaining money or asking for donations from the local community. Also, some clubs misuse their funding because they spend it without sufficient levels of accountancy and analysis. All 33 youth clubs (100 percent) expressed that they face financial issues in a program. Fund allocated for a programme is insufficient to address the needs of a larger community group. 78.79% of clubs stated that funds are not released on time.
b. **Management Issues**: Typically, the clubs don't have a Board. The difficulty of attracting members without paying them or offering them perks is one of the primary causes of this. Additionally, a sizable portion of clubs i.e. 23 (70 percent) do not believe governance is important for their organisations and lack a solid understanding of governance.
c. **Professional skills**: For the betterment of the community, clubs are founded with like-minded individuals, yet they typically lack professional expertise. Additionally, they

lack the operating budget to hire professionals to manage the initiatives. Therefore, a lack of professional expertise is troublesome as stated by all 33 youth clubs (100 percent).

d. **Sustainable development plan:** The issue of sustainability is important for growth because it calls for resource reserves. However, planning for sustainable growth becomes challenging due to a lack of accessible resources and capacity development as faced by 26 youth clubs (78 percent).

e. **Networking Issue**: It is challenging for 32 youth clubs (97 percent) to network with other organizations. Lack of resources result from an inadequate network with like-minded organizations, clubs, or individuals.

f. **Capacity development:** There is a need for capacity development of the members. The members join the club and activities are preformed but in order for effective and strategic implementation the capability building of the members becomes important which is usually lacking among 22 youth clubs (66 percent).

g. **Strategic planning**: The members usually make plans and implement the program but those lack strategic planning. As most of them are running it voluntarily, they do it on free time and that lacks strategic planning. A strategic planning involved professional commitment which is lacking among the members of 29 youth clubs (88 percent).

The youth clubs usually adopts some strategies to deal with those problems and challenges. Collected information in this regard is presented below.

- Guidance from mentors, NYK officials, other officials, and NGO management specialists
- Implementing activities that generate income,
- Finding the opportunities for the programme and source.
- Creating project proposals and submitting them to various departments,
- Fundraising efforts,
- Participating in training programmes for capacity development held by various agencies,
- Coordination with local government, participation in PRI training for NGO managers,
- Preparing Annual Reports,

As the study focuses on the youth clubs in rural community development and the clubs are operating in collaboration with both government and non government organizations, therefore the present study was conducted with one of its objective as to understand the role of Government and Non-Government organization for the promotion of the Youth Clubs in Gomati district of Tripura. Hence, the researcher had visited and consulted with many Government and Non Government organizations who are working with youth clubs are presented below.

## 5.8 Government Organizations Promoting the Youth Clubs

For the study, the researcher has interacted with the chief functionaries of the sixteen government organizations who are working with youth clubs to achieve different goals set for community development in the district. The consulted government organizations are as follows:

**Table 5.10: Govt. organizations consulted for the study**

| Sl. No | Organisation | Programme |
|---|---|---|
| 1. | Nehru Yuva Kendra | Skill development Training Programme |
| 2. | National Health Mission | Awareness programme on Cancer and Screening |
| 3. | National Bank for Agriculture and Rural Development | Skill development Training on Broom making, Paper bag making |
| 4. | Rural Self Employment Training Institutes | Training on EDP |
| 5. | Department of Agriculture & Horticulture | Awareness programme on FashalBimaYojana, Soil Health card schemes |
| 6. | Block development office | awareness programme on swacha Bharat Mission (SBM) like organising Rally, Miking, IEC distribution, Open defecation Free Block, Street play in Market, Schools, Door to Door campaign |
| 7. | Forest Department | 1000 sample plantation programme |
| 8. | Indian Institute of Entrepreneurship | Training on Youth Leadership and Community development programme(TYLCD) |
| 9. | Block Development Office | Tree plantation and Distribution, |
| 10. | Police Department | Prayas programme for mass awareness on importance of police & Different types of crimes. |
| 11. | Tripura State AIDS Control Society | Awareness programme on HIV/ AIDS |
| 12. | Skill Development Mission | Skill Development Training |
| 13. | Khadi& Village Industries Board | Awareness programme on Schemes of KVIB |
| 14. | District Administration | SBM awareness programme |
| 15. | Department of Fisheries | Fish Feeds and Seeds support Programme and Training to farmers for culture of fish in scientific line |
| 16. | Department of Agriculture | Awareness programme for farmers on different schemes of Agriculture department |

While interacting with the chief functionaries of the organizations, the researcher could understand that the select organizations are adopting diverse approaches for the promotion of the activities of the youth clubs. The findings are presented below

As the study focuses on the youth clubs in rural community development and the clubs are operating in collaboration with both government and non government organizations, therefore the present study was conducted with one of its objective as to understand the role of Government and Non-Government organization for the promotion of the Youth Clubs in Gomati district of Tripura. Hence, the researcher had visited and consulted with many Government and Non Government organizations who are working with youth clubs are presented below.

### 5.8.1 Role of Government Organizations for Youth Clubs Promotion

a. **Continuous engagement with programme implementation:** Different government organizations implements numerous community development programmes for the benefit of the community where youth clubs are engaged to maintain communication and lead role in mobilizing the community. This is how community people also come to know about the active role performance of the youth club.
b. **Partnering with Youth Clubs in survey**:Government organization conductssurvey on topic of importance time to time in which they involve youth clubs to reach out to the unreached and ensure authentic data.
c. **Market promotion development assistance**: GOs have different programs for market promotion. The youth clubs who work with SHGs, livelihood promotion and entrepreneurship are engaged with those programmes for creating an opportunity for marketing to the youth clubs which is contributing to their economic development.
d. **Develop capacities and skills of youth:** Government run different schemes for developing the skills and capacities of youths and also their training and placements. The youth clubs partners with govt. organizations are availing such services as per the requirement of the youth club.
e. **Advocacy and sensitization:** Government organisations of Tripura especially in Gomati district play advocacy role for the youth clubs. They advocates for the programs run by the youth clubs and sensitize the public to make use of the services offered by the youth clubs.
f. **Institution of Awards:** Government acknowledges the efforts undertaken by the youth clubs for community welfare through awards so that it enhances the performance of the youth clubs and set an example in the community.
g. **Meeting with youth clubs:** Government organizations like NYK periodically calls for a meeting with the youth clubs to monitor the activities and address any issues if

confronted by the youth clubs related to functioning and programme implementation of the youth clubs.

h. **Assistance with Publicity**: Government has wider reach out and thus shows supportive attitude to publicize the activities of the youth clubs and eventually make them partner for development which not only gain public support but also ensures better beneficiaries reach out.

## 5.9 Non-Government Organizations Promoting the Youth Clubs

Chief functionaries of the eighteen Non government organizations were consulted who are involved with youth clubs in delivering community development services together in the district. The consulted Non Government Organizations are as follows:

**Table 5.11: Non Govt. organizations consulted for the study**

| Sl. No | Organisation | Programme |
|---|---|---|
| 1. | Tata Trust | Awareness programme on SHG and Microfinance, different programme under Tata Thrust Agartala |
| 2. | Red Cross Society | Awareness on Disaster Management and DRR, First Aids Training |
| 3. | World Vision | Skill development Training programme |
| 4. | RRPC | Block level Youth Parliament, |
| 5. | AppoloMedskillPvt. Ltd | Awareness programme on Different Schemes and Benefits of Training Programmes |
| 6. | Kathia Baba Charitable Thrust | Skill development Training on Bamboo and Cane product |
| 7. | Jana ShikhaSansthan | Skill development Training |
| 8. | Nivedita Voluntary organization | Cancer screening camp and Awareness programme |
| 9. | North Eastern Handicraft Research Society | Skill Development Training Programme |
| 10. | piramal Foundation | Mega Health Check Up camp |
| 11. | Schedule Tribe welfare society of India | Awareness programme on Substance abuse |
| 12. | St.Vincent welfare Society | Awareness programme on diary Farming and Animal Husbandry |
| 13. | Voluntary Associationof Tripura(VHAT) | Awareness programme on Tobacco Control and Cancer |
| 14. | Disha Welfare Society | Awareness on DDUKVY training programme |

...

| | | |
|---|---|---|
| 15. | Entrepreneurship Development Society | Awareness on Income Generating Activities |
| 16. | Action Research and Training Organisation | Skill development Training |
| 17. | Agragami Social Organisation | Disaster Management Training and DRR, First Aids Training |
| 18. | Ashadeep | Awareness on Environment and Climate Change |

While interacting with the chief functionaries of the NGOs, it was observed that the organizations follow different approaches for the promotion of the youth clubs in the district. The findings are presented below.

### 5.9.1 Role of Non-Government Organizations for Youth Clubs Promotion:

a. **Organising programs in collaboration**: NGOs promote community development by putting into action plans that boost growth at the grass-roots level. In order to empower them as political players and engage with them for improving the community, NGOs specifically target a few youth clubs. Consequently, it is of the utmost significance that NGOs work with Youth Clubs to develop activities for young people.

b. **Developing awareness against social evils**: The next generation of leaders and decision-makers will be young people, thus it is crucial to build awareness campaigns to engage them in conversation about the significance of spreading concepts of social, economic, and political justice, human rights, and equality. NGOs inspire young people to fight social inequality and educate this generation on how to eliminate evils and create better ways of living. The rights and freedoms of all youth are promoted by NGOs, with a special focus on empowering groups that had previously been marginalized, such as young women and girls, people with disabilities, people living with HIV, people who are not in school, and people who live in rural regions.

c. **Providing education, training and technical assistance**: NGOs give villagers the chance to receive training that would prepare them for self-employment or better jobs. Through youth clubs, NGOs attempt to provide skill-based training to various segments of the population.

d. **Awareness generation:** NGOs and Youth Clubs work together to raise awareness of various social concerns as well as plans and initiatives that would benefit the neighborhood. NGO educates people, connects them to resources, and provides them with useful information through youth clubs.

e. **Creating Self employment or better employment opportunity**: NGOs undertake their activities to provide all young peoplethe chance of finding decent jobs and a sustainable means of livelihoodto increase the ability of youth clubs, as well as any other departments or organizations involved in youth affairs, to efficiently plan, carry out, oversee, and administer youth development services.

f. **Acting as social mediator:**Help young people acquire the knowledge, skills, and experiences needed to enable them to contribute productively to the growth of their country and society as a whole.

g. **Facilitating communication**: NGOs supplycurrent data on the country's youth development situation so that government organizations, non-governmental organizations, and the private sector can use it to form programme design, implementation, monitoring, and evaluation at all levels and in all sectors.

h. **Assistance with Publicity**: NGOsimprove communication and cooperation between key governmental, non-governmental, and community stakeholders while properly promoting the achievements of Youth Clubs.

   It has been understood that both GOs & NGOs are extending their support by making youth clubs a partner for implementing different programmes, conducting survey, market promotion; empowers youth for economic development; advocacy and sensitisation; institution of awards etc.

**Diagram 5.2 Role of Government organizations & Non Government Organizations – at a Glance**

**Role of GOs**

- Continuous engagement with programme implementation
- Partnering with in survey
- Market promotion
- Capacity development of Youths
- Youth Empowerment for Economic development
- Advocacy and sensitization
- Institution of Awards
- Meeting with youth clubs
- Assistance with Publicity

**Role of NGOs**

- Organising programs in collaboration
- Awareness generation
- Providing education, training and technical assistance
- Awareness generation
- Engaging in rural development works
- Employment Opportunities
- Social Mediator
- Facilitating Communication

**5.9.2 Expectation of Youth Clubs from Partner Organizations:** The youth clubs were interviewed regarding their expectation from the GOs and NGOS that will enable them in effective operation of the program and services. The expectations are recorded in chart 5.23.

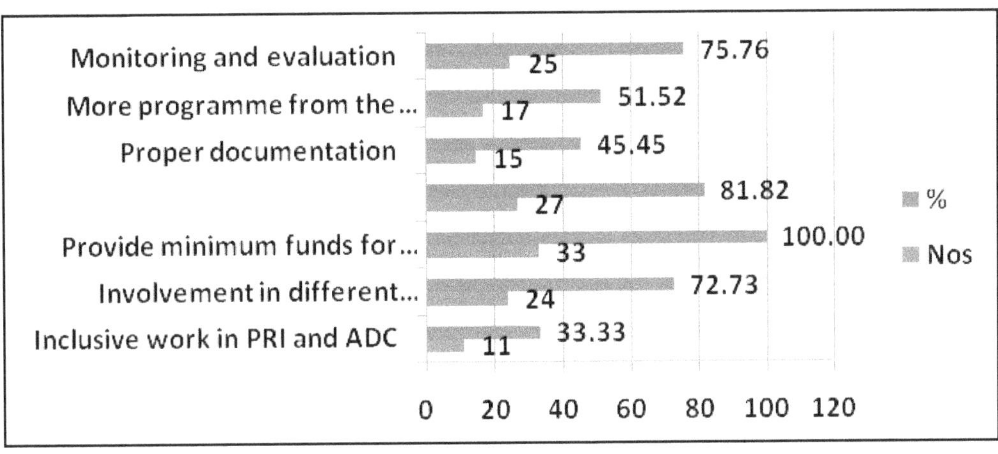


**Chart 5.23: Expectation from Partner organisation**

Chart 5.23 explains 33.33%(11) of the Youth clubs expects the GOs like District Administration for inclusive work in PRI, 45.45%(15) expects proper documentation support to all collaboration, 51.52%(17) expects more programs from NYK and other line departments, 72.73(24) of the clubs expects the district administration to be more involved at the grass root level while running any Govt. programs, 75.76%(25) of the clubs expects proper monitoring and evaluation support, 81.82%(27) of the clubs seeks support in training & youth Club management and 100%(33) of the Youth clubs seeks minimum fund to run office expense.

To understand the perception about the community people on the services and programs of the Youth club, 237 beneficiaries were interviewed. Before understanding the perception, the study first explored the demographic and socio-economic profile, which is presented below.

## 5.10 Demographic and Socio-Economic Profile

**5.10.1 Age of the Respondent:** The below chart shows the age wise classification of the respondents selected for the study. They were grouped into five age groups:15-24 years, 25-34 years, 35-44 years, 45-54 years and above 55 years. The chart 5.24 below depicts the respondents' age groups:

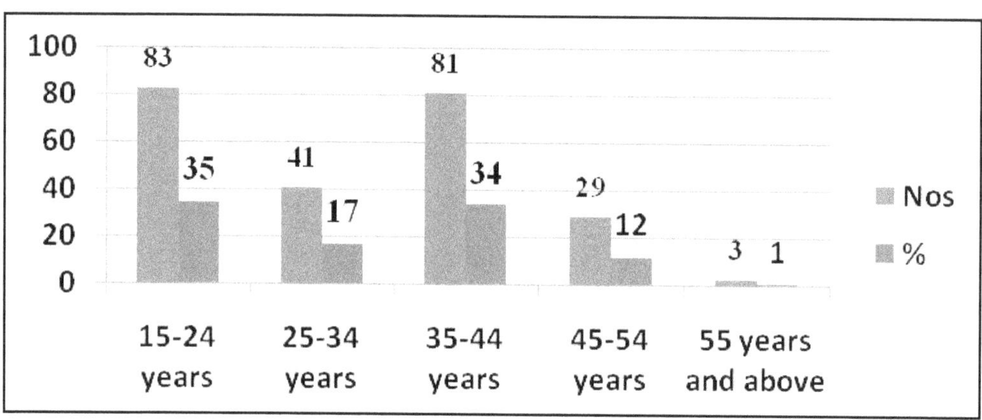


**Chart 5.24: Age of the respondents**

Chart 5.24, presented above shows that only 1%(3) of the respondents were from 55 years age group and above followed by 12%(29) from the ages of 45 to 54 years & 34%(81) were from the age group of 35 to 44 years, 17%(44) were in the ages of 25—34 years and 35%(83) from the respondents were from 15-24 years group. It emphasizes that majority of the respondents are from 15-24 years which mainly forms the youth group.

**5.10.2 Gender of the Respondent:** The below chart shows the gender wise classification of the respondents selected for the study. Different gender may have different perspectives of the situation. The below chart 5.25 depicts the respondents' age groups:

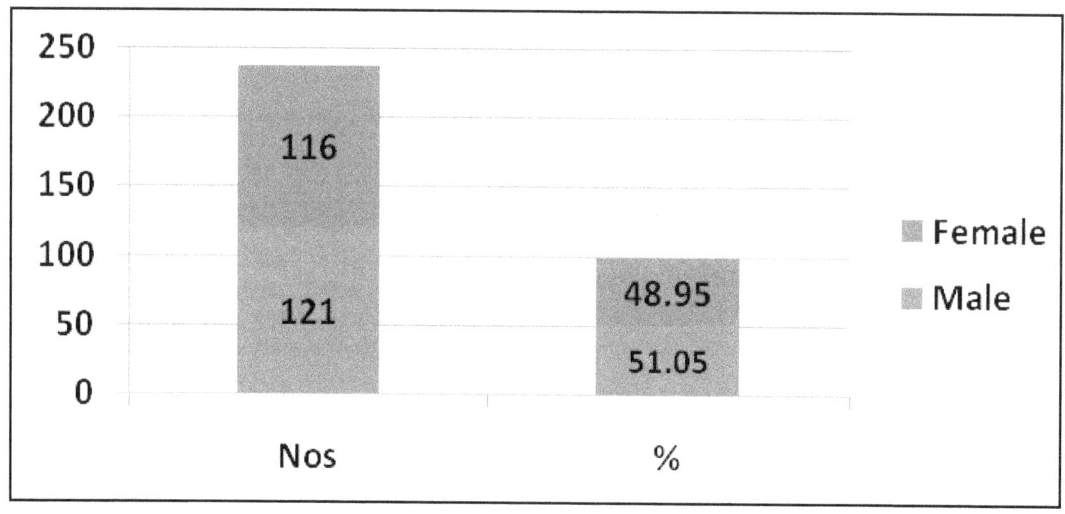


**Chart 5.25: Gender of the respondents**

Chart 5.25 shows that 48.95% (116) were female and 51.05% (121) respondents were male. So it explains that majority of the beneficiaries were male even though the female beneficiaries also form a good numbers comprising 48.95%.

**5.10.3 Category of the Respondent:**The below chart 5.26 shows the category wise classification of the respondents selected for the study. They were grouped into five major categories:Scheduled Caste, Scheduled Tribe, Other Backward Classes, General and Minority. The findings are presented below.

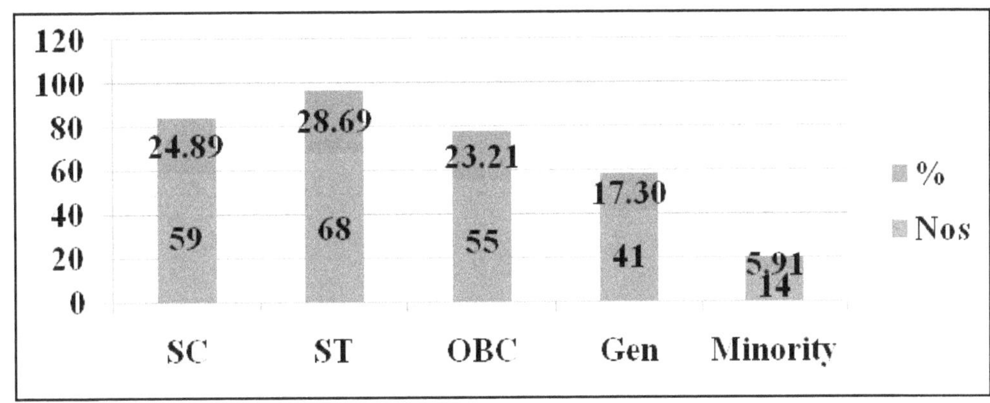


**Chart 5.26: Category of the respondents**

The statistical data presented in figure 5.26 shows that 24.89 percent of the respondents are from scheduled caste community while 28.69 percent belongs to Scheduled Tribe. 23.21 percent of the respondents are from Other Backward Community and 17.30 percent are from general category followed by 5.91 percent from minority. It indicates that majority of the respondents represented scheduled tribe but a considerable number is also representing Scheduled caste and other backward community.

**5.10.4 Education of the Respondent:** The following chart 5.27 presents the information about the educational status of the respondents. The educational standard has been categorized into six parts illiterate, Below HSLC, HSLC, HS, graduate, Postgraduate.

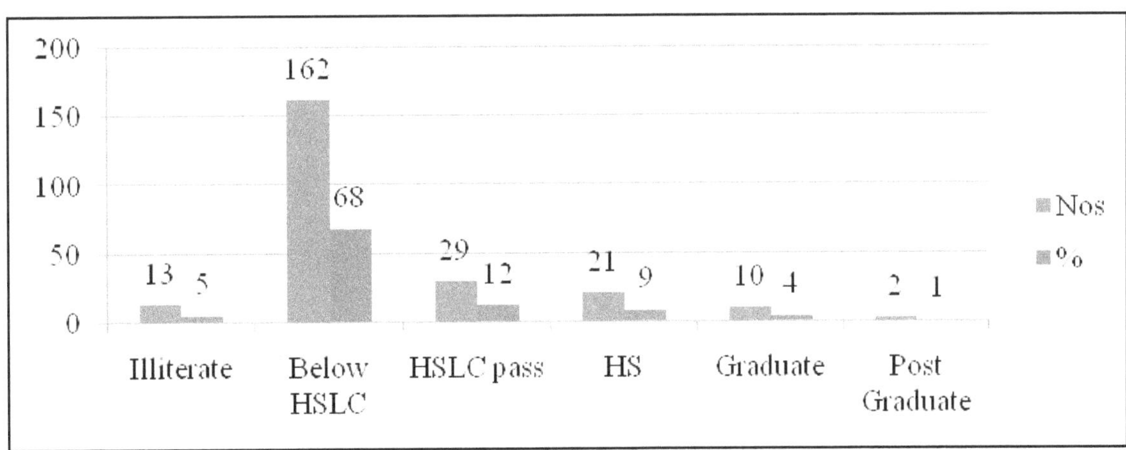


**Chart 5.27: Education of the respondents**

Chart 5.27 shows that, 1%(2) of them are post graduate, 4%(10) are graduate, 9%(21) are higher secondary pass, 12 %(29) of them are HSLC qualified, 35.02%(83) of them have studied till high school but not HSLC qualified, 68%(162) of them are below HSLC and 5% (13) of them are illiterate without any basic education. It indicates that most of the respondents who are also the beneficiaries are below HSLC.

**5.10.5 Economic profile of the respondents:** The economic statuses of the respondents who also form the beneficiary group were also studied. The economic status has been categorized in terms of their occupation and annual income. The social status of a family to a great extent is determined by their occupation. Good occupation gives a higher distinction in the society. With this background the present study intended to examine the relationship between the occupational background and the monthly income.Thus, accordingly the information has been collected and presented in chart 5.28.

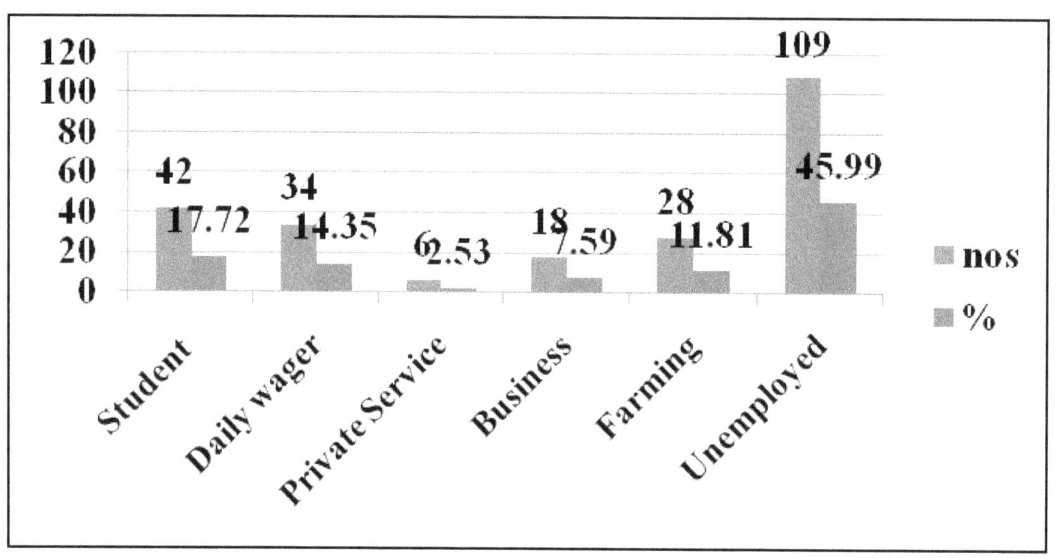


**Chart 5.28: Occupation of the respondents**

Chart 5.28 explains the occupational background of the respondents. 2.53%(6) of them has private jobs, 11.81%(28) of them are employed in agriculture, 14.35%(34) of them are involved as daily wage earners, 17.72%(42), of them are students and 45.99%(109) of the respondents that forms the majority are unemployed. The unemployed group comprises the students who just passed out and seeking jobs, the school drop outs and young generation and mostly the house wives.

**5.10.6 Monthly family income:** Since the majority of the respondents were unemployed, the family income was studied. The findings are explained below.

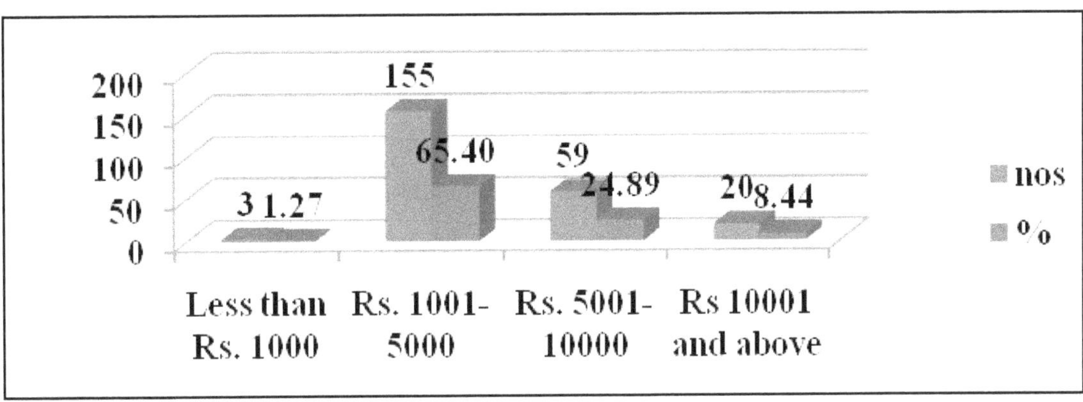


**Chart 5.29: monthly family income of the respondents**

Chart 5.29 states the family income of the respondents. Only 1.27% (3) of them have salary less than Rs. 1000, 8.44% (20) of them are having salary more than Rs.10000 but majority of the respondents i.e. 65.40%(155) have income between Rs. 1001 to Rs. 5000. So the respondents are not very high income group and have moderate income.

**5.10.7 Youth Club membership of the respondents:** To study the perception of the respondents, it was important for the researcher to know the membership status of the respondents. Therefore, the study put forth questions to the respondents to know whether they are members of the youth clubs receiving benefits or the only beneficiaries not the members of the club. The responses received from them are presented below.

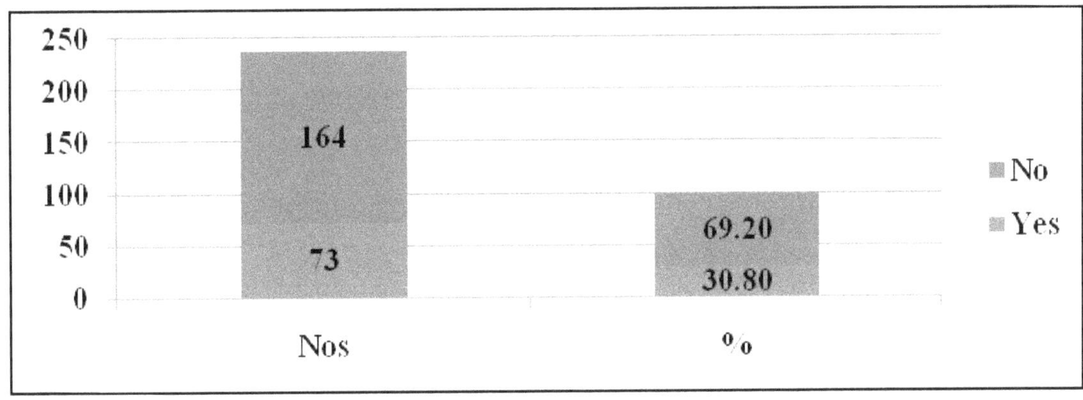


**Chart 5.30: Youth club membership**

The chart 5.30 shows that out of 237 respondents, 69.20% (164) did not have youth club membership and only 30.80% (73) were associated with different youth clubs of Gomati district of Tripura as members of that club. The data emphasizes that majority of the respondents who received benefits of different services provided by youth clubs are not members of youth clubs. Hence, the responses can be viewed as non-biased.

**5.10.8 Awareness about the core programs of the Youth Club:** The respondents were interviewed if they had information about the Youth Clubs. All the 237 respondents (100%) were aware about the existence of the youth Clubs through the members of the youth club, from the members of PRI and from a neighbor or relative. The reason stated was active involvement of youth clubs in rural community development initiatives. Any new initiatives in the rural areas are usually known to all the residents, said by the community people.

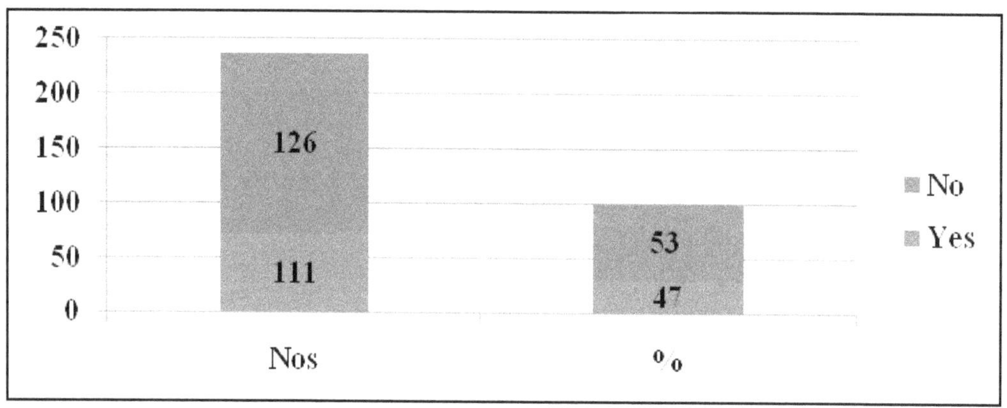


**Chart 5.31: Awareness on Core programs**

The above data presented in chart 5.31 indicates that out of 237 respondents 47 percent of the respondents were aware about the core programmes of youth clubs and 53 percent were unaware. On query study found that beneficiaries' who were members of different youth clubs within Gomati district of Tripura had better information in comparison to the non members of youth clubs regarding core programmes.

**5.10.9 Programme Beneficiaries:** The respondents were beneficiaries of various programs undertaken by the youth clubs and they were classified in accordance to the programmes, detail information in this regard is presented below.

**Table 5.12: Classification of respondents program wise**

| Sl. No | Name of Youth Club | Programme | Beneficiaries taken |
|---|---|---|---|
| 1. | Aranyak Club | Awareness programme on Cancer and Screening | 5 |
| 2. | Jewel Club | Skill development Training on Broom making, Paper bag making | 6 |
| 3. | Gomati SamajikSanghtha | Training on EDP | 8 |
| 4. | NabaudoiSangha | Awareness programme on FashalBimaYojana, Soil Health card schemes | 7 |

| | | | |
|---|---|---|---|
| 5. | Baishyamani Para sports club | Awareness programme on swacha Bharat Mission (SBM) like organising Rally, Miking, IEC distribution, Open defecation Free Block, Street play in Market, Schools, Door to Door campaign | 6 |
| 6. | Budhu Sadhu memorial Club | 1000 sample plantation programme | 4 |
| 7. | Teenmurty club | Training on Youth Leadership and Community development programme(TYLCD) | 9 |
| 8. | RRPC | Tree plantation and Distribution, | 5 |
| 9. | Evergreen club | Training on EDP | 7 |
| 10. | Brain Power Youth Society | Prayas programme for mass awareness on importance of police & Different types of crimes. | 6 |
| 11. | Boys student club | Awareness programme on HIV/ AIDS | 7 |
| 12. | Samai Club | Skill Development Training | 8 |
| 13. | Salka Club | Awareness programme on Schemes of KVIB | 8 |
| 14. | Kwthar Club | SBM awareness programme | 9 |
| 15. | Dharmangkur Youth Society | Fish Feeds and Seeds support Programme and Training to farmers for culture of fish in scientific line | 9 |
| 16. | Achin Baba Sangha | Awareness programme for farmers on different schemes of Agriculture department | 7 |
| 17. | Satadal play Centre | Awareness programme on SHG and Microfinance, different programme under Tata Trust Agartala | 5 |
| 18. | TarunSangha (Kusharghat) | Awareness on Disaster Management and DRR, First Aids Training | 8 |
| 19. | JatiaYuvaSanghstha | Block level Youth Parliament | 5 |
| 20. | Reformist Society | Skill development Training on Bamboo and Cane product | 9 |
| 21. | New star club | Cancer screening camp and Awareness programme | 10 |
| 22. | TarunSangha (Matabari) | Awareness programme on Substance abuse | 7 |
| 23. | Renessaiance Club | Awareness programme on dairy Farming and Animal Husbandry | 7 |
| 24. | Netaji Welfare Centre | Awareness on Income Generating Activities | 6 |
| 25. | DejayJodha Club | Awareness on Environment and Climate Change | 4 |
| 26. | Club Wasna | Mega Health Check Up camp | 8 |

...

| | | | |
|---|---|---|---|
| 27. | Swamiji Welfare Society | Awareness on Environment and Climate Change | 4 |
| 28. | Swamiji social welfare society | Awareness programme on FashalBimaYojana, Soil Health card schemes | 9 |
| 29. | Vivekananda club | Awareness programme for farmers on different schemes of Agriculture department | 8 |
| 30. | Red star club | Training on EDP | 10 |
| 31. | Nabashakti club | Awareness programme on Cancer and Screening | 8 |
| 32. | Eleven star club | Awareness programme on SHG and Microfinance, different programme under Tata Trust Agartala | 7 |
| 33. | Tiger sound club | Awareness on Disaster Management and DRR, First Aids Training | 9 |

## 5.11 Beneficiaries Perception about the effectiveness of the programmes

To understand the effectiveness of the programmes conducted by the youth clubs, the perceptions of the beneficiaries have been studied in two phases. First the researcher studied beneficiaries perception about the programmes implemented and secondly the perception was studied on the effects of those programmes in the study area.

For the first phase of data collection on perception, six parameters like relevance of the programme, appropriateness of the programme, equality for selecting beneficiaries, involving people in programme planning, meeting conducted for organizing programme have been identified and for the second phase of data collection, five parameters like social capital, social mobilization skills; capacity development; leadership development; socio-economic development were identified. The collected data on each parameter is presented in the below given tables.

**Table: 5.13: Beneficiaries perception about the programmes implemented**

| Sl.No | Parameters | Findings |
|---|---|---|
| 1. | **Relevance** of the program to community need | Majority of the respondents i.e. 51.90% (123) of the respondents feel the youth clubs are performing well in developing program relevant to community needs |
| 2. | **Appropriateness** of the Programs in context to community Situation | Majority of the respondents i.e. 45.57 % (108) considers the programs are appropriate in context to community situation |
| 3. | **Equality** maintained by Youth club in selecting beneficiaries | Majority of the respondents i.e. 49.37% (117) of the respondents feel the youth clubs are maintaining equality in selecting the beneficiaries'. |

| 4. | Involving community people in **Program planning** | Majority of the respondents i.e. 43.88% (104) of the respondents feel the youth clubs are performing satisfactory in involving community people in program planning. |
|---|---|---|
| 5. | Youth club **Programs benefitting the community** | Majority of the respondents' i.e.60.76% (144) of the respondents feel the youth clubs are performing well in implementing services that are benefitting the villages. |
| 6. | **Meeting conducted** with community people for program implementation | Majority of the respondents i.e. 70.46% (167) of the respondents feel the youth clubs are performing satisfactory in conducting meeting to involve the villagers in different stages of program planning. |

The above table indicates that the majority i.e. 51.90% of the respondents viewed that the programmesorganised for community development were relevant to the community situation. Further, 60.76% of the respondents expressed that the implemented programmes benefited them followed by 70.46% respondents expressed their satisfaction for involving community people in different phases of programme planning and thus initiatives of youth clubs made effective to the respondents.

### 5.11.1 Beneficiaries Perception about the Effects of the Programmes

**Effects of the Programmes:** The effectiveness of the programmes has been studied to understand the significant contribution made by the youth clubs through these programmes. The responses were recorded under the five parameters-social capital, social mobilization skills; capacity development; leadership development; socio-economic development. The finding of each parameter is presented below.

**Table 5.14: Effects of the programme**

| **Effects on** | **No. of Respondents(N=237)** | **Percentage** |
|---|---|---|
| Social Capital | 92 | 38.81 |
| Social mobilization skill | 108 | 45.57 |
| Capacity Development | 87 | 36.70 |
| Leadership Development | 73 | 30.80 |
| Socio-economic Development | 113 | 47.68 |
| Total | Not Applicable | Not Applicable |

The above statistical data presented in table 5.14 shows that38.81 percent of the respondents expressed that the programmes implemented by the youth clubs have improved their social capital; enhanced mobilization skills 45.57 percent; capacity development 36.70 percent and leadership development 30.80 percent followed by Socio-economic development 47.68 percent.

- **Effects on Social Capital**

**Table 5.15: Effects of the programme on Social Capital**

| **Social Capital (relational dimension)** | **No. of Respondents (N=237)** | **Percentage** |
|---|---|---|
| Social interactions | 97 | 40.92 |
| Social relationships | 104 | 43.88 |
| Social support | 92 | 38.81 |
| Total | Not Applicable | Not Applicable |

The table 5.15 shows that the programmes created a scope for the respondents to interact (41 percent) with each other and put forth their ideas which helped them in designing rules for the community where they seek to live. These programmes have also paved passage for building good relationships (43.88 percent) with one another and developed an attitude of extending social and emotional support (38.81 percent) which made the respondents more capable of dealing with problems efficiently.

- **Effects on Social Mobilisation:**

**Table 5.16: Effects on social Mobilisation**

| **Social Mobilisation Skill** | **No. of Respondents (N=237)** | **Percentage** |
|---|---|---|
| Explore community issues and set priority | 87 | 36.70 |
| Plan with the community | 92 | 38.81 |
| Evaluate together | 73 | 30.80 |
| Organise the community for action | 100 | 42.10 |
| Total | Not Applicable | Not Applicable |

The above table on 5.16 shows that 36.70 percent of the respondents expressed that the programmes implemented explored community issues, 38.81 percent expressed that al developmental works are planned with the community, 30.80 percent affirmed that the outcome of the program is evaluated along with the community people and 42.10 percent expressed the programs help in organizing the community for action.

- **Effects on Capacity development**

It is found that the programmes initiated by the youth clubs have significant contribution towards capacity development of the respondents. Therefore, it was interesting to know the aspects of capacity development. As per the data, the implemented programmes have developed the capacity of the respondents from two different perspectives like individual perspective & organizational perspective. The information has been collected accordingly and presented through below table 5.16.

**Table 5.17: Effects of programmes on capacity development**

| Capacity Development | No. of Respondents (N=237) | Percentage |
|---|---|---|
| Individual | 113 | 47.67 |
| Organisational | 124 | 53.32 |
| Total | 237 | 100 |

The table 5.17 presents that the 47.67 percent of the respondents viewed that different programmes made provisions to undergo training and thereby improved skills, built knowledge and gained experiences which developed their capacities at the individual level. Further, being a member of the youth club or programme organizing committee,53.32 percent respondents expressed that their capacity to run an organisation has developed as they were made acquainted with strategic plans, power structure, rules and regulations.

- **Effects on Leadership Development:**

The respondents viewed that getting engaged with rural development programmes benefited them in developing leadership qualities. Therefore, the researcher further intended to study the leadership aspects and collected information accordingly is presented below.

**Table 5.18: Effects on Leadership Development**

| Leadership Development | No. of Respondents (N=237) | Percentage |
|---|---|---|
| Effective Communication | 95 | 40.08 |
| Problem-solving skill | 111 | 46.83 |
| Management techniques | 62 | 26.16 |
| Total | Not Applicable | Not Applicable |

The statistical data presented in table 5.18 shows that 40.08 percent of the respondents viewed that their regular interaction with the youth clubs in different circumstances has improved their communication skills. 46.83 percent respondents are of the opinion that they inculcated problem solving skills in them and 26.16 percent of the respondents said that they have learnt the use of several management techniques accurately and make the condition better and better.

- **Effects on Socio-economic Development**

Though the programmes undertaken by the youth clubs were of very short duration yet it could reflect on some aspects of socio-economic development. Under the socio-economic parameter few sub parameters were identified to exactly figure out the effects of implemented programmes. The findings in this regard are presented below in table 5.19.

**Table 5.19: Effects of Socio-Economic Development**

| Social Development | No. of Respondents (N=237) | Percentage |
|---|---|---|
| Education | 200 | 84.38 |
| Health | 143 | 60.33 |
| Economy | 98 | 41.35 |
| Poverty | 77 | 32.48 |
| Income | 78 | 32.91 |
| Total | Not Applicable | Not Applicable |

5.19 table shows that 84.38 percent expressed that the programmes undertaken by the youth clubs had immensely benefited the community to understand the need of promotion of education. The programmes had equally addressed the health issues of different age groups 60.33 percent. Different programmes related to poverty alleviation has contributed towards income generation of 32.91 percent of the respondents, improved the social status of 32.48 percent rather economic status of the 41.35 percent respondents.

The above data on beneficiaries perception about programme implemented indicates that out of six parameters, three parameters (Relevance of the programme to community need; Youth club Programs benefitting the community; Meeting conducted with community people for program implementation) could ensure positive response from majority of the respondents (more than 50 percent) and the other 3 parameters (Appropriateness of the Programs in context to community Situation; Equality maintained by Youth club in selecting beneficiaries; Involving community people in Program planning) ensured the responses of respondents which is below 50 percent.

## 5.12 Beneficiaries Suggestions for Improvement of the Programmes

The beneficiaries perception about the effects of the programmes implemented were studied on the five parameters (Social Capital; Social mobilization skill; Capacity Development; Leadership Development; Socio-economic Development). The five parameters were again divided into sub parameters. After analyzing data on each parameter, it is found that the community people perceived most of the programmes as effective one.Further, the majority of the respondents, i.e. 78 percent expressed their satisfaction with regards to the services provided to them by the youth club members. It was equally interesting to know that 100 percent of the respondents supported the formation of the youth clubs for the greater benefit of the local area development. The data explains that the youth clubs of Gomati district are working well for the rural community upliftment.To maintain the pace their work the respondents proposed the following suggestions.

1. Youth Club objectives to be decided after need assessment of the community and resource mapping.
2. Need assessment and resource mapping to be conducted only after stakeholders meeting.
3. The stake holders meetings must consist of representatives from different segments of the population like women, youth, aged etc.
4. Proper proposal may be prepared and funding support to be sought in consultation with district administration to either government or NGOs or corporate.
5. Skilled people or localities having professional qualification may be a part of the meeting who will set the goals for the clubs.
6. The goals must be doable and the resources available must be taken into consideration while setting the goals.
7. Along with resources, the environment supporting the goals must also be taken into consideration.
8. The goals must be respectful towards community culture and must invest in building social capital.
9. Liasoning and networking must be an important agenda if the youth clubs needs to grow and sustain.
10. The goals must be set such that each activity must ensure maximum community participation.

# Chapter – 6

# Concluding Discussion

In India, youth clubs act as a catalyst for change in the development of rural communities. In developing nations like India, youth clubs work with youth and community members to carry out a variety of programmes and services in the community. Youth clubs engage in a variety of activities, including encouraging youth to volunteer, disseminating educational and career development programmes, promoting agriculture and rural self-employment, livelihood initiatives, disaster management, swachata Evam Shramdaan, sports culture, traditional culture promotion, skill development and life skill, and more.

Tripura attained complete statehood in January 1972. The District had five (5) Subdivisions and eleven (11) Development Blocks as of the 2011 Census. With effect from January 21, 2012, the South Tripura district has been split into the eight-block South Tripura District and the eight-block Gomati District. According to the 2011 Census, the district has a total population of 876001, with men making up 51% and women 49%, respectively. A total of 14% of the population lives in cities, while 86% of the population lives in rural areas. According to the 2011 Census, there are 2.53 lakh people in the age range of 15 to 29 years, with 1.27 lakh men and 1.25 lakh women.

910 youth clubs in Tripura are affiliated with NYKS, Tripura (according to online registration under NYKS), including those in North Tripura (279), West Tripura (239), Dhalai (148), and South Tripura (356), according to online statistics from youth clubs affiliated with NYKS, Tripura. To comprehend the role of youth clubs in various parameters, such as the role of youth clubs in community development, the role of NGOs in community development, and the relationship between CBOs and community development, various works of literature were examined.Community development is now recognised as a dominant strategy in social development, according to Gaik (1981). Practices for community development create social capital, aid in the growth of engaged citizenship, and offer an option to passive welfare.

Establishing rural youth clubs in the village is one of the successful strategies used to organise rural youth, as Singh (1983) emphasised in his study. The five benefits of Nonprofits in providing services for India's rural development are discussed in Ramakrishna H.'s (2013) article. In addition to government interventions, a variety of roles that are flexible, locality-specific, felt need-based, beneficiary-oriented, and committed have been created.

According to the reviewed literature, community development is a series of initiatives planned specifically at the local level to raise the quality of living for residents in all spheres (Social, economic, political). Community development strategies include leading change through dialogue, collaborative leadership, and collective empowerment. The literature on NGOs showed that because of their distinctive qualities like independence, responsiveness, efficiency, and adherence to participatory approach, NGOs are thought to be the primary initiators of grassroots level development.

The summary of the literature suggests that, despite being more community-centered and locality-specific than NGOs, youth groups are unable to have an impact on the community through their activities. The literature shows that the various research studies that have been conducted have mainly dealt with the function, significance, and assessment of CBOs' contributions to various fields of development. In order to close the gap between youth clubs and rural community development in Gomati District, Tripura, the present research work focussed on the role of youth clubs based on rural development indicator. This is because the review of literature does not fully express how CBOs' work is based on rural development indicators.

The study was hence conducted to understand the youth club and their role in community development. The study was conducted with four main objectives, viz, a) To understand about the programmes implemented by youth clubs for the community development of the area. b) To study the problems and challenges encountered by the youth clubs in implementing the programmes, c) To understand the role of the GOs and NGOs for the promotion of the youth clubs in the area, and d) To study the beneficiaries perception about the effectiveness of the programmes conducted by the youth clubs for rural community development.

The findings and discussions of the study were interpreted through different charts and tables that explain the Youths clubs and their relation with rural community development in Gomati district of Tripura. The study identified that despite the district having a large number of clubs that have already been established, more work needs to be done to formalise the clubs for better organisation.For the past 40 years, youth empowerment has been occurring in the Tripura district of Gomati. However, the majority of clubs only felt the need to formalise their operations 6–10 years after their founding, despite the fact that clubs were founded and operating efficiently in the Gomati district as early as the 1980s.

The study explains the various beneficiary groups that the youth clubs are dealing with in great detail. Each club works with multiple beneficiary groups. The data explains that 100% of the youth clubs work for youth development. The research explains that the services offered by Achin Baba Sangha, Aranyak Club, Samai Club, and Jewel Club have the greatest impact on the community. The studywas also able to observe that while Samai and Jewel have been in operation for a long time and were founded in 1984 and 1992 respectively, Achin Baba and Aranyak were founded in 2002 and 2004 respectively. Achin and Aranyak have therefore accomplished the most in comparison to the groups that are the oldest despite having less time to do so.

The research reveals that the majority of the club's members, out of 1755 people who belong to 33 NGOS, are either farmers or students. According to the survey, 63.64% of the youth organisations worked with line departments. The Nehru Yuva Kendra, Block Development Office (BDO), RSETI, SBM, Tata Foundation, Panchayat, MLA Fund, cooperative society, NABARD, KVIC, Banks, CSR Fund, and others are among the main line organisations.

The study unequivocally proves that all 33 youth clubs (100%) maintain their books of accounts. Among the most popular books of records are the case book, bank book, stock book, audit report, and other books of records. Although every youth organisation in the Gomati Districts of Tripura maintains financial records, the bulk of them are not audited. The study found that while some of the 33 youth clubs got funding from NGOs for different projects, all 33 were independently managed and funded by the government.

The research found that sports and awareness-raising initiatives are the main priorities of all 33 youth organisations in the Gomati district. These are the primary pursuits of the study's target youth organisations. According to the study, while 54.55% (18) of the youth clubs claimed that the panchayat has no involvement in their programmes, 45.45% (15) of the youth clubs claimed that the panchayat has involvement in the programmes, either in planning, implementation, or funding. The biggest barrier to the clubs' growth is the absence of consistent funding, despite the fact that they are working for the community. This is evident from the fact that the majority of club members only attend activities when it is convenient and possible for them to do so.

The study found that while some organisations claimed to rarely receive assistance, it wasn't delivered on time. Very few organisations have the ability to mobilise their own resources; the majority are completely dependent on their partner group. These clubs only exist because of the community's support and participation in club events. For the community's benefit, clubs are established with like-minded individuals, but they typically lack professional expertise.

The clubs require assistance from a number of stakeholders in order to operate. With this background knowledge, the third goal attempted to comprehend the GOs' and NGOs' role in the promotion of youth club. The findings presented that along with financial support, both GOs & NGOs provides networking support by promoting the youth clubs in different ways like – conducting meetings with youth clubs, publicise youth club activities, posting of govt. notices in clubs, making youth club members as the members of the district advisory committee for youth development programmes, and connecting youth clubs with social media for assistance are the ways of promoting youth clubs.

In order to learn more about how the community members viewed the Youth club's services and activities, 237 beneficiaries were surveyed. The majority of respondents, who range in age from 15 to 24 and 35 to 44, are young individuals. Although there were a significant number of female beneficiaries, generally there were more male beneficiaries.

The study explains the beneficiaries' degree of satisfaction with the Youth clubs' services. The recipients were grateful for the help with village development, rural community growth, and other services, such as those that promote communal harmony and peace. The youth club organised skill-building and other training programmes for village kids. Residents are encouraged to volunteer by the youth club. Youth clubs improved the social well-being of the community. The community is informed about the major government initiatives by the youth group. Youth organisations urge youngsters to add to the social wealth of society by their developmental activities.

It is evident from the study that youth clubs are a strong pillar to respond to the needs of the community thereby promoting rural community development. Thus, the study leaves room for developing youth groups and formalizing them so that numerous worthwhile projects and appropriate funding can be accessed for community development. Further research on the inactive youth clubs may be conducted with an objective to understand the causal factors responsible for making the clubs inactive and propose suggestions for making them active.

# Bibliography


Abegunde, S.M. (2009). Key message on meningitis. The antecedents and consequences of community engagement strategy. *Journal of Public Health*, *17*, 23-41.

Albal, D.R., & Koujalagi, N.Y. (2018). Challenges of Rural Youth Today. *Aayushi International Interdisciplinary Research Journal*, *5*(1).

Aminu, A. A. (2012). Youths and community development in nigeria. *Journal of Educational and Social Research*, *2*(7).

Ani, A.O (1999). Toward Rural Development: A conceptual Model for Rural-Urban Balance in Nigeria. In; Undiandeye, U.C, Bila, Y and Kushwaha, S. SustainableAgricultural Development. Principles and Case Studies in Nigeria. Maiduguri. Mainasara Publishing Company

Banajawad,V.T., & Adi,Dr.M.S.(2021). Role of Youth in Rural Development.*Universe International Journal of Interdisciplinary Research*, *1*(8), 188–195. https://doi.org/http://www.doi-ds.org/doilink/01.2021-73989868/UIJIR

Barnett, R. V., & Brennan, M. A. (2006). Integrating youth into community development: Implications for policy planning and program evaluation. *Journal of Youth Development*, *1*(2), 16. https://doi.org/10.5195/jyd.2006.382

Bhaskar, I and Geethakutty, P. (2001), Role of Non-Government Organizations in Rural Development: A Case Study, *Journal of Tropical Agriculture*, *39* (1), 52-54.

Brennan,M. A.(2006).The development of community in the west of Ireland: A return to Killala twenty years on. *Community Development Journal*, *42* (3), 330 – 374.

Brennan, M. A., Barnett, R. V., & Lesmeister, M. K. (2007). Enhancing Local Capacity and Youth Involvement in the Community Development Process. *Community Development*, *38*(4), 13–27. https://doi.org/10.1080/15575330709489816

Brennan,M. A.(2008).Conceptualizing resiliency: An interactional perspective for community and youth development. *Child Care in Practice Building—Resilience in Children, Families, and Communities*, *14*(1), 55–64.

Brennan,M. A., & Luloff, A. E.(2007). Exploring rural community agency differences in Ireland and Pennsylvania. *Journal of Rural Studies, 23* (1), 52 – 61.

Bwala, M.H. and Aminu, A. (1996). —Community Development and Rural Transformation in Nigeria.‖ Educational Forum. A Journal of Educational Studies; Vol. 2, No. 2.

Chauke, T. A., & Malatji, K. S. (2021). Qualitative Study on Challenges Faced by Professional Youth Workers in South Africa Africa. *African Journal of Development Studies, 11*(3), 31–53. https://doi.org/10.31920/2634-3649/2021/v11n3a2

Community Services & Learning, *Michigan State University Extension 4-H Youth Development* (Accessed 01/2014).

Crossouard, B., Dunne, M., Szyp, C., Madu, T., &Teeken, B. (2022). Rural youth in southern Nigeria :Fractured lives and ambitious futures. *Journal of Sociology, 58*(2), 218–235. https://doi.org/10.1177/14407833211042422

Devi,L.(1997). *Rural development finances and technology*. Anmol Publisher.

Dhesi, A. S. (2000). Social capital and community development. *Community Development Journal, 35*(3), 199–214. https://doi.org/10.1093/cdj/35.3.199

Dolidze, S. (2021). *The Situation of Youth Organizations in Georgia*. National Council of Youth Organisation in Georgia. ISBN: 978-9941-8-3438-7.

Durston, J. (1999). Building community social capital.*69*, 103–117. https://hdl.handle.net/11362/10700

Eriksen, I. M., & Sel and, I. (2021). Conceptualizing well-being in youth: The potential of youth clubs. *Young, 29* (2), 175–190. https://doi.org/10.1177/1103308820937571

European Union & Council of Europe. (2014). *Revisiting youth participation: Current challenges, priorities and recommendations*. European Union.

Fukuyama, F. (1996). *Trust: The social virtues and the creation of prosperity*. Simon and Schuster.

Halstead, J. M., Deller, S. C., & Leyden, K. M. (2022). Social capital and communitydevelop ment:Where do we go from here? *Community Development,53*(1),92–108. https://doi.org/10.1080/15575330.2021.1943696

Hillman,A. (1960): Community Organisational Planning. New York: Macmillan.

Huber, M. S. Q., Frommeyer, J., Weisenbach, A., & Sazama, J. (2003). Giving youth a voice in their own community and personal development: Strategies and impacts of bringing youth to the table. In F. Villarruel, D. Perkins, L. Borden, & J. Keith, *Community Youth Development: Programs, Policies, and Practices* (pp.297– 324). SAGE Publications, Inc. https://doi.org/10.4135/9781452233635.n14.

IFAD.(2019).*2019 Rural Development Report: Creating Opportunities for Rural Youth*. Creating Opportunities for Rural Youth; International Fund for Agricultural Development. https://www.ifad.org/ruraldevelopmentreport.

Ismail, M. (2001). *Community Development: Distance Education Module*. Institute for Distance Education, University Putra Malaysia, Kuala Lumpur.

Jain,G.L.(1997). *Rural development*. Mangal Deep.

JoAnne Schneider. (2004).*The Role of Social Capital in Building Healthy Communities*. Annie E. Casey Foundation.

Jones, G. E. (1981). The origins of agricultural advisory services in the nineteenth century. *Social Biology and Human Affairs, 46* (2), 89-106.

Kay, A. (2006).Social capital, the social economy and community development. *Community Development Journal*, *41*(2), 160–173. https://www.jstor.org/stable/44258961.

Kiilakoski, T., & Kivijärvi, A. (2015). Youth clubs as spaces of non-formal learning: Professional idealism meets the spatiality experienced by young people in Finland. *Studies in Continuing Education*, *37*(1), 47–61. https://doi.org/10.1080/0158037X.2014.967345.

Kumar, A. (1981). Principles and Practice of Adult Education and Community Development. *Ibadan. Abprint Publishing Company Limited*.

L. Bestul, —*How Youth Participation Benefits Adults and Organizations,*‖ Youth-Adult Partnership in Community and Government(12/2012).

Labonte, R. (1999). Social capital and community development: Practitioner emptor. *Australian and New Zealand Journal of Public Health*, *23*(4), 430–433. https://doi.org/10.1111/j.1467-842X.1999.tb01289.x

Laksmana, C. and B.Vijaya Mohan. (1968). A Study of the Working of the Rural Youth clubs. *Indian Journal of Extension Education*, *4(*1-2), 89-94.

Letlhaku, L. L. M., & Letlhaku, L. L. N. (1961). Problems of youth clubs—Some solutions. Community *Development Bulletin, 13*(1), 17–22. https://www.jstor.org/stable/44279328

Luloff, A. E., & Bridger, J. (2003). Community agency and local development. *Challenges for rural America in the twenty-first century*, 203-21.

Mandalu, M. P. (2023).*Exploring core 5 roles of youth on rural development in their country.* LinkedIn; LinkedIn. Retrieved September 11, 2023, from https://www.linkedin.com/pulse/exploring-core-5-roles-youth-rural-development-mandalu-ph-d

Mayo, S.C. (1958). An approach to the understanding of rural community development. *Social Forces*, *37*(2), 95–101.https://doi.org/10.2307/2572790

McGrath, B., Brennan, M. A., Dolan, P., & Barnett, R. (2009). Adolescent well-being and supporting contexts: A comparison of adolescents in Ireland and Florida. *Journal of Community & Applied Social Psychology*, *19*(4), 299-320.

Nitzberg, J. (2005). The meshing of youth development and community building. *New Directions for Youth Development*, (106), 7-16.

Obot, I. D. (1989). Rural development programme of the DFRRI in Cross River: A pessimistic view. *Journal of the Institute of Town Planners*, *8*(10).

Olatunbosun, D. (1977). Crisis in development. *Keynote Address to Rural Development at Village level in Savannah Environment of Nigeria. ENDA (UN). Dakar and CAEES. Zaria. Ahmadu Bello University.*

Opare, S. (2007). Strengthening community-based organizations for the challenges of rural development. *Community Development Journal*, *42*(2), 251–264. https://doi.org/10.1093/cdj/bsl002

Opare, S. (2007). Strengthening community-based organizations for the challenges of rural development. *Community Development Journal*, *42*(2), 251–264. https://doi.org/10.1093/cdj/bsl002

Pearce, J. (2000). *Development, NGOs and civil society*. Oxfam GB.

G.(Eds.),*Community youth development:Programs, policies and practices*. (pp. 1 – 23). Thousand Oaks, CA: Sage Publications.

Pittman,K. J.(2000).Balancing the equation: Communities supporting youth, youth supporting communities. *Community Youth Development Journal*, *1*, 33 – 36.

Plows, V. (2010). Challenging interactions: An ethnographic study of behaviour in the youth club. https://era.ed.ac.uk/handle/1842/5847

Prajapati, V., & Patel, B. (2011). Constraints faced by the Tribal youth while participating in the Rural Development Activities in Banaskantha District. *Gujarat Journal of Extension Education*, *22*, 87–89.

Purao,P. (2000). Poverty Alleviation & Empowerment Measures, *Social Welfare*, *47*, 25 – 28.

Putnam, R. D. (1994). *Making democracy work: Civic traditions in modern Italy*. Princeton Univ. Press.

Pyakuryal,K.(1970).Community development as a strategy to rural development. *Occasional Papers in Sociology and Anthropology*, *3*, 58–68. https://doi.org/10.3126/opsa.v3i0.1076

Rajasekhar K. (1987). Involving rural youth in developmental activities. *Kurukshetra*, *25*(9), 8-9.

Amamurthy,A.(2006).The politics of britain's asian youth movements. *Race& Class*, *48*(2), 38–60. https://doi.org/10.1177/0306396806069522.

Rubenson, D. (2005, June). Community Heterogeneity and Political Participation in American Cities. Canadian Political Science Association meeting, London, Ontario. https://cpsa-acsp.ca/papers-2005/Rubenson.pdf

Rubin, H. J. (2000). *Renewing Hope within Neighborhoods of Despair: The Community – based Development Model*. Albany, NY: Sate University of New York Press

Saikia, P. K. (2015). Role of Non-Governmental Organisations in Rural Development: A Case Study. *Social Science Journal of Gargaon College*, *3*.

Scales, P.C.,& Leffert, N.(1999). *Developmental assets*. Minneapolis, MN: Search Institute.

Shukla BD. (1971). People's participation in community development programme. *Rural India*, *34*(9), 187–190.

Singh, K N. and K Kumar. (1977). Interest Pattern of Rural Youth, *Indian Journal of Extension Education*, *13* (1-2).

Singh, K.N. and C. Prasad. (1963). Rural Youth Clubs. A Case Analysis, *Kurushetra*, *12*(2), 17-20.

Singh, R. (1983). Extent of Participation in Projects by the Members of Rural Youth Club in Iraq. *Indian Journal of Social Research*, *24*(3).

Williams, T., McCall, J., Berner, M., & Brown-Graham, A. (2022). Beyond bridging and bonding: the role of social capital in organizations. *Community Development Journal*, *57*(4), 769-792. https://doi.org/10.1093/cdj/bsab025.

Tiwary, S. N., & Prajapati, S. N. (2011). Role of NGO in Rural Development: A Case Study of R.K. Mission (KVK) in Ranchi District. *Jharkhand Journal of Social Development, 4*(2).

Tripathi,H.,Dixit,V.,Singh,S.,Yadav,R.,&Sing,I.(2018).An Analysis of Causes for Rural Youth Migrations. *Indian Journal of Extension Education*, *54*(3), 53–58.

United Nations (1963): Report of the Conference on National Development, by an Adhoc Group of Experts appointed by the Secretary General of the U.N. New York.

Wattar, L., Fanous, S., & Berliner, P. (2012). Challenges of youth participation in participatory action research: Methodological considerations of the Paamiut youth voice research project. *International Journal of Action Research*, *8*(2), 185-212.

Youth Voice research project. International Journal of Action Research,8(2), 185–212.

Wilkinson, K. P. (2023). *The community in rural America*. University Press of Colorado

# Annexure A-I: Interview Schedule for Youth Clubs in Rural Community Development

## Section A: Profile of the Youth Club

1. Name of the Youth club
2. Office Address & Contact No
3. Name of the Block
4. Genesis of Youth Club
5. Vision of the Youth Club
6. Mission of the Youth Club
7. Objective of the Youth Club
8. Year of establishment
9. Date of Registration
10. Date of affiliation under NYK
11. Registered under
12. Administrative Set up of the Youth Club:
13. Area of Operation: a) Urban b) Rural c) Tribal d)Both
14. Target Population
15. Sources of Fund
    a. Self generated (MembershipFees)
    b. Government(Central/ State)
    c. NGO
    d. Others (Please Specify)
16. Nature of Beneficiaries

17. Area of Coverage
    a. Total number of Villages/Para
    b. Total number of Community
    c. Total Population
18. Does the club have its office in the village

    Yes/ No

    If Yes, Types of office

a) Own Building b) On Lease c) Rented d) Part of village Asset e) Rent free building

**Section B:Profile of youth club members**

19. Total member of the Youth Club
20. No.of women members
21. No.of male members
22. Caste wise members in the youth club
23. Age category of Members

    a) 15-19 b) 20-24 c) 25-29 d) 30-35 e) 36-45 f) 46 – above

24. Major occupations of youth club member?

    a) Job b) Business c) Daily wager d) Cultivator e) Student
    f) Housewife g) Unemployed

25. Monthly income of the members:

**Section C: Accounts & Record Maintenance**

26. How do you maintain Account Records?

    a) Cash Book b) Bank Book c) Ledger d) Stock Book
    e) Trial Balance f) Audit Report

27. How do you maintain members & programme records?

    a) Meeting Register b) Membership Register c) Programme and Activities register
    d) Beneficiary Register e) Any other

28. Whether youth club is audited?

    a) Yes b) No

    If yes, when did last audit take place?

**Section D:PreparationofActionPlan/Report/ Assessment**

29. Do you prepare Annual Action Plan?

    a) Yes    b) No

30. What process does the youth club follows to prepare the Action Plan?

    a)

    b)

    c)

31. Do you prepare activity reports?

    a) Yes    b) No

    If yes,    a) Monthly    b) Quarterly    c) Yearly

32. Do you make self assessment of your work?

    a) Yes    b) No

    If yes,    a) Monthly    b) Quarterly    c) Yearly

**Section E: About the Programmes**

33. What are the programs implemented by the youth club?

**I. Programmes implemented for individual development**

a. Capacity Building activities
b. Vocational training and guidance
c. Income generation programme
d. Life skill education and training
e. Survival skills training
f. Health programmes
g. Sports activities
h. Art & culture activities, etc.

**II. Programmes for Community Development**

i. Awareness Generation (EDP, Tree Plantation, HIV)
j. Block level youth parliament
k. Observation of special days
l. Agriculture and allied activities

m. Education and general knowledge – education
n. Economic and Income Generation Activities – MSME
o. Shram dhans
p. Swacha Bharat-PHE
q. Swachaata Hi Seva
r. Environmental Sustainability---Forest Dept., Govt. of Tripura tree plantation
s. Disaster Preparedness---NYKDDMA
t. Health activities-NHM
u. Hygiene & Sanitation
v. National Integration/Communal Harmony
w. Promotion of Sports & Games
x. Promotion of Art & Cultural Activities
y. Social Service
z. Participation in Local Governance
aa. Coordination & Networking
ab. Training in Life Skills and Survival Skills :NYK()
ac. Youth Information Centre: self defense course
ad. Advocacy Activities :NYK:
ae. Blood donation camp
af. Sports programme
ag. Sishu Mela
ah. Wash Training programme

34. Duration of the programme:
35. Funding agency of the programme:
36. Total sanctioned amount for the programme:
37. Nature of activities under the programme:
38. Role of youth club under the programme:
39. How does the youth club select the programme
    a. Identification of the need of the community
    b. Prioritizing the need of the community
    c. Any Other (Please specify)

40. Procedure for acquiring Government-sponsored programmes
    a. Responding to Advertisement
    b. Proposal submitted with interest
    c. Investigation or Scrutiny by funding agency
    d. Youth functionaries are called for interview
    e. Agreement/Bond is signed
    f. Project is sanctioned
    g. Any other
41. Procedure for acquiring NYK – sponsored programmes
    a. 3 months work experience with NYK before affiliation
    b. Affiliation under NYK
    c. Submission of 3monthlyactivityreporttoNYK
    d. Account details along with audit report if any
    e. Consideration by District Youth Officer & National Youth Volunteers.

**Section E:Coordination with other departments**

42. Does the youth club have coordination with the line department?

    a) Yes b) No

If yes, what are those?

| | | | | |
|---|---|---|---|---|
| a) Nehru Yuva Kendra | b) Agriculture dept. | c) Health dept. | d) Fishery dept. | e) Youth affairs and Sports fund |
| f) Block Development Office | g) RSETI | h) SBM | i) Tata Trust | j) Panchayat |
| k) MLA Fund | l) Cooperative Society | m) NABARD | n) KVIC | o) Banks |
| p) CSR Fund | q) Others. | | | |

43. Is there any involvement of PRIs in programme implementation?

    a) Yes b) No

**Section F:Funding Process**

44. Funding process by the funding agency
    a. 1$^{st}$instalment
    b. Utilisation Report

c. Review of Report

d. Monitoring by funding agency

e. 2nd Instalmentiffoundeverythingasper guidelines

45. Funding process of NYK

a. Sanction letter

b. Submission of statement of expenditure with original bills

c. Submission of Report

d. Release of total fund

**Section G: Reporting & Monitoring**

46. Do you need to report the progress of the work?

a) Yes b) No. If yes, to whom and how frequently?

47. How often are the reports being sent?

48. Do you receive reply after sending a report?

a.Yes b. No c. Sometimes

49. Who monitors your progress of work?

a) Self b. Team c. Reporting Head d. Higher Authority e. None

50. Are you doing Programme-wise reporting under NYK?

a) Yes b) No

51. What are the indicators followed while reporting?

a. Programme Budget

b. Training module

c. Programme activities

d. Documentation

e. Problem and Challenges

f. Expectation of the Trainee/Youth Clubs Members

g. Suggestions if any

h. All of the above

52. What monitoring process do you follow?

a. Monthly review meeting in your office

b. Weekly review meeting with the collaborative agencies

c. Constitution of the project monitoring committee who sit periodically

d. Any other, please mention.

53. What monitoring process does NYK follow?

a. Monthly review meeting of NYV and Youth club executives under NYK
b. Visit to the programme site by the State Director and Senior officials of NYK
c. Half-yearly meeting with DACYP chaired by Deputy Commissioner
d. Constitution of programme Monitoring committee under Chairmanship of District Youth Officer, NYK
e. Regular field visits in sponsored programme site under NYK in the District

# Annexure A-II: Interview Schedule for the Youth Clubs in Rural Community Development

## Section A:Implementationof the programme

1. Number of programmes implemented with the cooperation of NYK during the study period
2. Number of programmes implemented with the help of other agencies
3. Number of programmes implemented by Youth Club by its resource mobilization
4. Number of programmes implemented by youth clubs depending on external financial resources

## Section B:ProblemsandChallengesencountered

### Problems

### A. Staff/Member

5. Do you have sufficient staff/member to run the activities of youth club?

   a) Yes  b) No

6. Do the members perform their designated roles?

   a) Yes  b) No

7. Do the members feel motivated to work for the community?

   a) Yes  b) No

If no, please mention he reasons

8. Do the members committed to achieve the objectives of the youth club?

   a) Yes  b) No

9. Are the chief functionaries able to blend members of different personalities into a cohesive and unified team?

   a) Yes  b) No

10. Does youth club get support from their own office staff for the successful implementation of the programme?

    a) Yes b) No

**B. Community Mobilization**

11. Can youth club mobilize community people to make the programme successful?

    a) Yes b) No

12. Can youth club mobilize own resources successfully to make the programme successful?

    a) Yes b) No

13. Do you think that youth club has necessary skills and behavior to ensure people's participation?

    a) Yes b) No

14. Are the community people responding to the initiatives of youth clubs?

    a) Yes but not always b) No

15. Do you get a satisfactory response from community people after the successful implementation of the programme?

    a) Yes b) No

**C: Coordination & Cooperation**

16. Dothemembersofyouthclubsharesresponsibilityformakingtheprogramme successful?

    a) Yes b) No

17. Doestheyouthclubreceivesufficientcoordinationfromthelinedepartmentsto ensure the program's successful implementation?

    a) Yes b) No

18. Are the funding agencies responsive to youth clubs' inquiries?

    a) Yes b) No

**D. Financial Aspect**

19. Is the amount sanctioned for the programme sufficient?

    a) Yes b) No

20. Do you receive the full sanctioned amount before the programme?

    a) Yes b) No

If not, how do you manage the programme?

21. Is the fund released timely?

    a) Yes  b) No

22. Does the youth club have sufficient balance in the account to run a programme?

    a) Yes  b) No

**E. Monitoring & Evaluation Process**

23. Does the funding agency monitor the progress of the work as per timeline?

    a) Yes  b) No

24. Does the funding agency share their observation during monitoring?

    a) Yes  b) No

If yes, what mechanism the club follows for further improvement of the activities

25. Does youth club assess the program's effectiveness?

    a) Yes  b) No

**Challenges**

26. What challenges does the youth club confront?

a) The issue of fund; b) The issue of management; c) The issue of strategic planning; d) Plans for sustainable development e) The issue of governance; f) The issue of networking g) The issue of professional skills; and h) The issue of transparency

27. What challenges youth club face in delivering services to the community people?

    a)
    b)
    c)
    d) Any other (Please Specify)

28. Has NYK been informed about the problems & challenges faced by the youth club?

    a) Yes  b) No

    If yes, what was NYK's response?
    If No, why have you not discussed with NYK?

29. What approaches/strategies does youth club follow to overcome the problems & challenges?

30. Any suggestion for improving the programme implementation process.

# Annexure A-III: Interview Schedule for GOs &NGOs

**Section A: Role of Govt. and Non Govt. organizations**

**Section A:Profile of the Organisation**

1. Name of the Organisation:
2. Office Address & Contact No:
3. Vision:
4. Mission:
5. Objective:
6. Target Population:
7. Area of operation/coverage:

**Section B:Aboutthe programs**

8. What are the programs implemented by the organisation?
9. What criteria do you follow to select youth clubs?
10. Are the youth clubs active in community work?

    a) Yes b) No

    If not, what demotivates the youth club?

**Section C: Role of Government Organisation & NGOs for youth club promotion**

**Role of Government Organisation**

a. Continuous engagement with programme implementation
b. Partnering with GOs in survey
c. Financial support provided to maintain sustainability
d. Market promotion development assistance
e. Develop capacities and skills of youth
f. Mobilizes, motivates, and activates rural youth

g. Empowers youth for economic development
h. Advocacy and sensitization
i. Constitution of area-wise Village Committees
j. Establish institutional mechanism
k. Institution of Awards
l. Meeting with youth clubs
m. Assistance with Publicity
n. Member of District Advisory Committee for Youth Development Programmes
o. Assistance with social media
p. Other (specify)

**Role of NGOs for youth club promotion**

a. Organising programs in collaboration
b. Developing awareness against social evils
c. Guiding to undertake activities and training to address social evils
d. Enable and educate the youth clubs in enhancing the awareness
e. Engaging in rural development works
f. Creating Self employment or better employment opportunity
g. Acting as social mediator
h. Facilitating communication
i. Building community participation
j. Mobilizing local resources
k. Providing education, training and technical assistance
l. Bridging the gap
m. Monitoring& Evaluation

# Annexure A-IV: Interview Schedule for Beneficiaries'

**Section A:Demographic & Socio-Economic Profile**

1. Name
2. Age :
3. Gender :
4. Marital status
5. Caste/Class :
6. Religion :
7. Education:
8. Occupation :
9. Type of Family :
10. Annual Family income :
11. Other sources of income, if any :

**Section B: Awareness about youth club**

12. How did you come to know about the youth club?
    a. From the members of the youth club
    b. From the members of PRI
    c. From a neighbor or relative
    d. Others (Please specify)
13. Are you a member of the youth club?
    a) Yes b) No
14. Are you aware of the core programs of the youth club?
    a) Yes b) No

15. Are you aware of the duration of these programs?

    a) Yes  b) No

16. Have you been involved in any of these programs?

    a) Yes  b) No

## Section C: Beneficiaries Perception about the Effectiveness

### I. Beneficiaries Perception about the programmes implemented

A. Relevance of the programme

17. Was the programme relevant to the community?

    a) Yes  b) No

B. Appropriateness of the programme

18. Was the programme appropriate in context to the community situation?

    a) Yes  b) No

C. Marinating equality in selecting beneficiaries

19. Did the youth club maintain equality in selecting beneficiaries?

    a) Yes  b) No

D. People's involvement in programme planning.

20. Does the youth club involve community people in programme planning?

    a) Yes  b) No

E. Conductance of meeting before implementing the programme

21. Does the youth club conduct meeting with the community people before implementing the programme?

    a) Yes  b) No

F. Youth club Programs benefitting the community

22. Aretheprogrammesimplementedbyyouthclubsbenefitingthecommunitypeople?

a) Yes b) No

**Beneficiaries Perception on the Effects of the Programmes**

A. Social capital

(i) Social interactions
(ii) Social relationships
(iii) Social Support

B. Social mobilization skills

(i) Explore community issues and set priority
(ii) Plan with the community
(iii) Evaluate together
(iv) Organise the community for action

C. Capacity development

(i) Individual development
(ii) Organisational development

D. Leadership development

(i) Effective Communication
(ii) Problem-solving skill
(iii) Management techniques

E. Socio-economic development

(i) Education
(ii) Health
(iii) Economy
(iv) Poverty
(v) Income

23. Do you think there is a need to having a youth club in a community?

    a) Yes b) No If yes, explain why?

24. Analyse youth club from a SWOT perspective
25. Any suggestion for future goal setting of the youth club.

www.ingramcontent.com/pod-product-compliance
Ingram Content Group UK Ltd.
Pitfield, Milton Keynes, MK11 3LW, UK
UKHW062008290726
14090UKWH00022B/1446